# BEYOND BARS

## REJOINING SOCIETY AFTER PRISON

### JEFFREY IAN ROSS, Ph.D., and
### STEPHEN C. RICHARDS, Ph.D.

**ALPHA**

A member of Penguin Group (USA) Inc.

## ALPHA BOOKS

Published by the Penguin Group

Penguin Group (USA) Inc., 375 Hudson Street, New York, New York 10014, USA

Penguin Group (Canada), 90 Eglinton Avenue East, Suite 700, Toronto, Ontario M4P 2Y3, Canada (a division of Pearson Penguin Canada Inc.)

Penguin Books Ltd., 80 Strand, London WC2R 0RL, England

Penguin Ireland, 25 St. Stephen's Green, Dublin 2, Ireland (a division of Penguin Books Ltd.)

Penguin Group (Australia), 250 Camberwell Road, Camberwell, Victoria 3124, Australia (a division of Pearson Australia Group Pty. Ltd.)

Penguin Books India Pvt. Ltd., 11 Community Centre, Panchsheel Park, New Delhi—110 017, India

Penguin Group (NZ), 67 Apollo Drive, Rosedale, North Shore, Auckland 1311, New Zealand (a division of Pearson New Zealand Ltd.)

Penguin Books (South Africa) (Pty.) Ltd., 24 Sturdee Avenue, Rosebank, Johannesburg 2196, South Africa

Penguin Books Ltd., Registered Offices: 80 Strand, London WC2R 0RL, England

*To Stephen Colbert, who teaches us that maintaining a sense of humor is perhaps the best piece of advice when you are faced with tough times.*

# Contents

# Appendixes

# Foreword

I am honored that the authors have asked me to write this foreword to their latest book. I remember when Jeffrey Ian Ross and Stephen Richards co-authored their second book together, *Convict Criminology*. When it came out in 2003, I was so impressed with the book that I asked them for copies I could distribute to Congress and Directors of the Federal Bureau of Prisons. *Convict Criminology* was about ex-convicts becoming criminology professors.

In 2002, Ross and Richards' *Behind Bars: Surviving Prison* was published. That book immediately became one of the most popular books available on going to and surviving jail and prison. Now, they follow up with a companion book for ex-convicts returning to the community. Both books follow Joe and Jill Convict as they struggle to learn from their mistakes and turn misfortune into a better future.

*Beyond Bars: Rejoining Society After Prison* also "comes out" of prison. One of the co-authors spent time in nine different federal prisons. The other author worked in a correctional institution for close to four years. This book traces the steps of Joe the everyman and Jill the everywoman as they exit prison to reenter society.

For the past 36 years my wife Pauline and I have been the co-directors of Citizens United for the Rehabilitation of Errants (CURE), an international organization dedicated to the reduction of crime through the reform of the criminal justice system (especially prison reform). We believe that a person is sent to prison as punishment, not for punishment. Once they get to prison, they should not be beaten or abused.

The goals of CURE are these: (1) Prison should be used only for persons who absolutely must be incarcerated, and (2) Prisoners should be given all the necessary resources they need to change their lives.

There are CURE chapters in most U.S. states and several countries. CURE now has more than 20,000 members worldwide.

Membership includes prisoners, their families, correctional workers, and activists in the community.

When Pauline and I began our grassroots organization in Texas in 1972, it was not uncommon for prison staff to say to people being released, "See you later." When we expanded to become a national organization in 1985 and moved our headquarters to Washington, D.C., we discovered that this anti-correctional attitude permeated most prison systems, even though it was not as "in your face" as in Texas.

The Federal Bureau of Prisons and state prisons have pre-release and reentry programs. In the past they used to give a few dollars of gate money to prisoners so they could buy lunch on the way home. If an inmate was lucky, they might even be given a bus ticket home and "free-world" clothes to wear instead of their prison jumpsuit. Pauline tells the story of once taking a bus from a correctional facility and sitting next to an ex-convict who had just been released and had already bought "a bottle" with the few dollars he received.

The reentry movement is long overdue. In fact, if you review the "prisoner" movies from the James Cagney gangster films to *Shawshank Redemption,* you will see the crucial need for providing help to released prisoners. For years, common sense dictated that this was a problem. However, we didn't have the political will to begin to address the solution that we now call "reentry."

When Jeremy Travis, then with the Urban Institute, released a report at a news conference in 2004, it was the first time I had ever heard the word "reentry" being used in relation to people released from prison. In fact, someone suggested changing the word because "it connotes returning from outer space." But then everyone present seemed to realize that this is exactly what people coming out of prison and back to the community were experiencing.

Next, Gene Guerrero entered the "reentry movement." The Open Society Institute, in Washington, D.C., part of the Soros Foundation, had hired him to do criminal justice reform. Guerrero, a longtime advocate for social issues on Capitol Hill, was assigned to coordinate a reentry coalition of organizations advocating congressional legislation on reentry. I was honored to represent our organization in this ad-hoc group.

In January 2004, it was beginning to look like our work was paying off: President George W. Bush, in his annual State of the Union message, said that people in prison should return to society better than when they went in. Thus, the name "Second Chance" originated with Bush's speech. We made progress when the Second Chance Act (SCA) was introduced by Rep. Danny Davis (D), and Rep. Rob Portman (R) in the House, and by Sen. Sam Brownback (R) and Sen. Joe Biden (D) in the Senate.

The SCA includes funding for services intended to help people coming out of prison. Driving this legislation is the fact that over 600,000 people are released from our nations' correctional facilities every year. Public safety will be substantially enhanced when we reduce the numbers of people being returned to prison. The House of Representatives voted overwhelmingly, 347 to 62, to pass the Second Chance Act in the 110th Congress. The Senate followed the House's lead and it was finally signed into law by President Bush on April 9, 2008. At the signing, President Bush humbly talked about his past drinking problem and his need for help to successfully overcome it. He concluded by saying that "government has a responsibility to help prisoners to return as contributing members of their community. In other words, we're standing with you, not against you."

The SCA is meant to address our urgent need to support men and women coming out of prison. Spending nearly $30,000 per year to keep one person in prison is simply too expensive. We need a national conversation to address ways to help formerly incarcerated people become productive citizens. As a nation, we cannot afford to fail.

*Beyond Bars: Rejoining Society After Prison* was written to help prisoners find a way home. This book provides valuable lessons on how men and women might successfully exit prison and reenter society. Written to help people coming out of jail and prison, the authors map out the journey home and provide helpful advice.

Ross and Richards are both professors of criminology and criminal justice. Their writing is based on their research and real-life experience. They provide a comprehensive overview of the problems prisoners face when they leave jail or prison. Then they give practical examples for how these problems can be solved, obstacles overcome, and a new life constructed. *Beyond Bars* is the book that we all need to read.

—Charlie Sullivan, Director, Citizens United for the Rehabilitation of Errants (CURE)

# Introduction

The United States has the largest population of prisoners in the world. When we take a look at the statistics, the numbers are downright scary. Approximately 7 million people (juveniles and adults) are in some form of correctional custody. Of those people in custody, 2.3 million are in jail and prison, another 4.2 million are on probation, and 784,000 are on parole. Add to this 15 million more people who are arrested each year and spend one or more days in jail.

This means that hundreds of thousands of people are released from city and county jails each month, and over 600,000 men and women leave state and federal prison each year. Recent estimates indicate that there are 30 million convicted felons living in the United States today.

From 1980 to 2000, the nation's prison population increased by a whopping 500 percent. As of 2008, 1 out of every 100 adults age 20 to 40 was in prison. Men are 10 times more likely to be in jail or prison than women. Over 90 percent of the people behind bars are men.

We are locking up young men, especially African Americans and Hispanics, at an alarming rate. Behind bars we find 1 in 100 white men over age 18, and 1 in 15 black men over age 18. This means that African American men over age 18 are nearly 7 times as likely to be in prison as white men.

## The Perpetual Incarceration Machine

In 1992, we first referred to the criminal justice system as a "perpetual incarceration machine." Our intention was to describe how the system continues to grow because of its failure to reform or rehabilitate inmates. Convicted defendants go to prison, do their time, get out, spend a few months or years on the streets, and then return to a correctional facility. Nearly 50 percent of new admissions are people who have previously served time; in effect, the same individuals are being "recycled" again and again. Most men and women who go back to prison do so for parole violations. A smaller number are convicted of new crimes.

Almost every time they return to prison they become more alienated, angry, and anti-social. Eventually, one of two outcomes is predictable: either they give up and make a home for themselves behind bars, or they "go warrior" and decide that the next time they get out nobody will send them back.

Prison has a strange way of converting relatively mild-mannered, peaceful men and women into desperados who would rather shoot it out with law enforcement than return to the penitentiary. They turn "outlaw" because they know they "can't make it" on the outside and they no longer care what happens to them or anyone else in the community.

The sad part is that the criminal justice machinery depends upon a growing inmate population to guarantee continued funding and employment for correctional facilities and their staff. Criminal justice employees, including law enforcement officers, lawyers, judges, correctional officers and administrators, and probation and parole agents, depend upon a growing population of defendants and prisoners to maintain their employment, gain promotion, and advance their careers. The more arrests, convictions, and inmates, the more job security for people employed by the system.

From 1980 to 2000 the number of prisons grew by 300 percent, with new facilities popping up all over America. Prisons are so prevalent that airplane pilots can navigate their way at night by the high-powered security lights of these institutions. From a distance, a prison might look like a new factory. Up close, however, you can see the security perimeter, with razor wire and gun towers, and realize that it must be a penal facility. If it's a minimum-security institution, such as a work camp, prison farm, or work release center, you might mistake it for a corporate warehouse, light industry factory, or office complex.

Many states have prison towns with two or more facilities. Some states have built correctional complexes with four prisons on the same property, each housing 5,000 to 6,000 inmates. These are usually on the outskirts of small towns where the prisons are the major employer.

The U.S. government has built mega correctional complexes all over the country. Nearly the entire local economy in towns like Leavenworth, Kansas; Florence, Colorado; and Coleman, Florida, depends upon the prisons, with correctional facilities employing thousands of staff and contracting with many local businesses.

As the global economy expanded, factories closed and family farms disappeared in these rural communities. In response, the local politicians allowed or even encouraged federal or state governments to build correctional facilities. Some communities invited private prison corporations to do the same. Now, former factory workers and farmers work for the county, state, or federal government correctional institutions. They wear neatly pressed uniforms, drive new pickup trucks, and count the years until they can cash in their retirement funds and collect their government pension. You can see them in the morning at the local café eating breakfast and slamming down cups of coffee before they report to work. They no longer talk about the weather or the price of fertilizer. Sometimes they smile, but none of them are in a big hurry to report to the prison. They have learned that managing convicts is less fun than manufacturing products, herding livestock, or driving tractors.

Meanwhile, state governments are shifting funding from education and highways to pay for construction and operation of these penal facilities. This means that your local schools don't get repaired, potholes don't get fixed, and your community has to raise your property taxes to pay for the incarceration of more prisoners. The rule of thumb is that it costs $20,000 (minimum-security camp) to $80,000 (supermax prison) per year to keep one man or women behind bars. Welcome to the perpetual incarceration machine. The real horror of the system is that it is recycling the same people. The person goes to prison, gets out, comes home, and then eventually goes back. Some waste their early adult years, and others spend their whole lives caught in the system.

We know from history that soldiers coming home from war, be it Vietnam, Iraq, or Afghanistan, often have a difficult time reentering society. Convicts recently released after serving lengthy prison terms experience similar problems. They, too, have lived for years in "harm's way." Large numbers suffer from post-traumatic stress disorders (PSTD), where they have trouble sleeping, eating, or carrying on casual conversation. Many of these men and women have serious problems finding suitable housing and employment and are also suffering from chronic or acute medical and psychological issues. They are banged up, weary, and exhausted, although they are also initially optimistic that the worst is behind them and better days lie ahead.

Whatever their crimes, prisoners pay big-time for their transgressions. After years behind bars, they return home to live among us as our neighbors. As people with a prison record, their lot is not easy. A felony conviction marks men and women for life. Still, like the rest of us, they need a place to call home, a job to pay their bills, somebody to care about, and a way to fit in and be accepted. If they fail, they return to prison, or end up derelict or destitute, fed and clothed by either the taxpayer or charity. The human wreckage piles up on ghetto street corners and accumulates in homeless shelters.

With a little help and a lot of luck, they might still find a way out of the perpetual incarceration machine. We hope this book helps them to make their way as they search for answers to the many challenges they confront.

## Who Can Benefit from This Book

Building on our first book, *Behind Bars: Surviving Prison* (Alpha, 2002) we introduce you to *Beyond Bars: Rejoining Society After Prison*. This is a practical handbook for people who are currently incarcerated in, or have recently been released from, jail or prison.

As scholars, instructors, activists, and citizens, we care about the communities we live in. Unfortunately, all across this country there is a dramatic tragedy unfolding before our eyes. Men and women get out of jail or prison just to be returned within a few weeks, months, or years. We know that when most people exit a correctional facility they want to do good, but for reasons beyond their control or their skill sets, they commit new crimes or somehow violate the conditions of their parole, and are sent back to prison. If only they had better information, and were more realistically prepared, maybe then they would have better odds of beating the perpetual incarceration machine.

In addition to convicts in jail and prison preparing for release and their families and loved ones, criminal justice practitioners, like probation and parole officers, and lawyers, can use *Beyond Bars* as a source of practical information and tips for people being released from correctional facilities and reentering society. This includes preparing for release, life on the streets, and how to survive the ordeal of parole, or what is now called "community custody." We also hope our advice can help community activists, planners, teachers, social workers, and college admissions officers as they confront the reentry problem in their communities. Others who may benefit from reading *Beyond Bars* include defendants in criminal court proceedings, convicted felons who have only served probation, ex-convicts living in free society, their families and friends, prison case managers, correctional officers, teachers, chaplains, clergy, and prison reform activists.

## A Source of Reliable Information

The majority of books about probation and parole are written for college and university classroom use. These are generally written for a student audience by people who typically have very little first-hand experience with prisoners and parolees.

Almost all so-called "self help" books on reentry have been written by ex-convicts and are out-of-date and hard to locate. Our hope is to fill the gap by providing reliable, easy-to-understand, practical information and advice for ex-convicts and the people who care about them.

## Our Reason for Writing This Book

Our purpose in writing this book is to help the people who need it the most: prisoners who are about to be released or have recently been released from jail or prison. The practical, hands-on advice might well give them the tools and information they need to know to avoid being arrested again.

Finally, please note that we cite many examples in this book. These stories are based on composites rather than any specific individuals. Any similarity to people living or deceased is purely coincidental.

## Acknowledgments

This book, like our previous work, is a truly collaborative effort. As such, we would like to thank our agent Jake Elwell, of Harold Ober Associates, for negotiating the contract; Paul Dinas at Alpha Books for adopting and shepherding this book; Jennifer Moore for development matters; and Janette Lynn and Jan Zoya for their editorial expertise.

We would like to thank our students for listening to parts of this manuscript as lectures. We would also like to acknowledge what we have learned over the years from our many Convict Criminology colleagues and friends, including but not limited to: Leanne F. Alarid, William Archambeault, Bruce Arrigo, James Austin, Thomas J. Bernard, James Binnal, Todd Clear, G. David Curry, Jeff Ferrell, Mark S. Hamm, Keith Hayward, Richard Hogan, Alan Hornblum, Jay Hurst, Ekunwe "Silver" Ikponwosa, John Irwin, Robert Johnson, Richard S. Jones, Michael Lenza, Shadd Maruna, Alan Mobley, Daniel S. Murphy, Greg Newbold, Barbara Owen, Hal Pepinsky, Chris Rose, Dawn L. Rothe, Randall Sheldon, Pauline and Charlie Sullivan, Richard Tewksbury, Jim Thomas, Loic Wacquant, Michael Welch, and Barbara H. Zaitzow.

Finally, we would like to extend our appreciation to our immediate families who have always been there for us. Jeff wants to thank Natasha, Keanu, and Dakota; and Steve wants to thank Donna, Andre, Jan, and Brian.

# Chapter 1

## Preparing for Release from Prison

If you're like most convicts, you've spent a lot of your time in the joint fantasizing about what your life will be like when you finally get out. Perhaps the first thing you plan to do is eat a good meal at your favorite restaurant, or make love to your spouse, hug your kids, or even just walk outside at night and look up at the starry sky.

Beyond those first few days of freedom, you've probably imagined getting a fresh start. Having served your time, you hope that people—including your family, friends, and neighbors—will give you a chance to prove that you are a new man or woman, ready to put your past behind you.

*This time* you are going to stay straight and focused and make something of yourself. You're going to repair your strained or shattered family relationships and make up for lost time with your kids. After you're on your feet again, with a decent job and a nice place of your own, you might even go to night school and get a college degree. Who knows, maybe someday you'll even go on that African safari or Caribbean cruise you've always dreamed about.

Unfortunately, without proper preparation for life on the outside, even the most optimistic and determined of ex-convicts can stumble, fall flat on their face, and end up back in the joint. In our introduction to this book, we noted the dismal statistics, but they bear repeating: *almost half of all the folks entering prison are people who have already done time.*

Why do so many ex-convicts fail to succeed? You can bet it's not because they plan to or want to. Despite everything, most people walking out of jail or prison are wildly optimistic. They are convinced that this time everything will fall into place and that their luck has changed.

A big part of the reason ex-convicts end up back in the joint is that nobody ever fully informed them of the perils that await them on their return to the streets. And they also fail to take into account how life on the inside has changed them.

You see, although time has seemed to stand still for you, out in the real world people have moved on. Your friends on the outside haven't been sitting around waiting for you. They've gotten married, started families, gotten divorced, and made new friends. If your buddies were leading lives of crime, perhaps your conviction scared them straight, and they want nothing to do with you now that you are out, for fear of getting into trouble.

Your family, sick with worry about you, but also angry at you for all you've put them through over the years, might not be willing to give you a second, sixth, or fifty-fifth chance. Your girlfriend or wife might have found someone new on the outside to give her the comfort and support she had always wanted from you. And even if your spouse has remained loyal, it's going to take some effort to rekindle the love and trust you once had. Your kids, who have only seen you a few times in the last decade, might not know how to act around you. They might even be embarrassed to be seen with you.

And as for that great job, working the grill at the Burger Barn wasn't really what you had in mind. Your weekly paycheck is hardly enough to cover your grocery bills, let alone your rent. And you have no idea how you're ever going to pay that back child support you owe. Faced with this grim economic reality, you find yourself tempted to go back to your old ways, where the money was easy and you never had to ask, "Do you want fries with that?"

So here's our first piece of advice: don't expect that any part of being free is going to be easy, at least not at first. As a matter of fact, it's going to be damn hard. You will be tempted to return to your old ways—drinking, using drugs, being a criminal—time and time again.

The good news is that by reading this book, you're putting yourself in a position to beat the odds. That's because we tell you the truth about what you can expect on the outside, and we offer practical advice for succeeding in situations where all too many ex-convicts fail. We give you a plan for a successful reentry.

Of course, we can give you all the information and advice in the world, and it's still not going to make a difference unless you make the tough choices to stay clean, stay disciplined, and stay away from trouble.

Everyone deserves a second chance. Our goal in this book is to help you make the most of it.

## Meet Joe and Jill Convict

Throughout this book, you'll follow the story of two fictional inmates, Joe and Jill Convict, as they begin their journey from prison back to the street. These characters represent the men and women who are sentenced and do time in America's jails and prisons.

Joe, Jill, and their fellow inmates have spent months in jail or years—sometimes most of their adult lives—locked up in penitentiaries or correctional institutions. Many of them were first confined as teenagers or young adults. Now much older, they are set free to make their way in society again.

## Prisons Are an Artificial World

Convicts live in a tightly controlled environment, far removed from what lies beyond the tall fences or high walls. This is an artificial world, with a very different social system than on the outside.

Depending on the length of time spent in the joint, prisoners may have little memory of what passes for everyday social conventions in the outside world. They may be shy or withdrawn and unable to carry on a normal conversation. The longer people are inside, the more acclimated they will be to the routine of prison time, and the more difficulty they may have readjusting to daily events on the street.

In penitentiaries, convicts wear the same clothes, eat the same food, and for the most part have the same daily schedule. Everybody gets up at the same time each morning, goes to bed at the same hour at night, and nobody is allowed outside after the sun goes down. You can spend years in prison and never see the moon or stars.

## Joint Mentality

Prisoners develop what's often called a "joint mentality," which affects the way they walk and talk. Because their lives are so structured and almost entirely out of their control, ex-convicts often suffer from an altered perception of time and an inability to plan a coherent future. Many people living outside prison walls take their freedom for granted, a luxury denied to the ex-convict, whose joint mentality causes him to live day to day, like he did in confinement, without anticipating or planning future events.

As a prisoner you forget the obligations and responsibilities most people shoulder. You do not pay for housing, food, or transportation. No car to fix, gas to buy, monthly bills to pay, or income taxes to file. Moreover, there is no family to care for, children to raise, or parents to bury. Your day-to-day life does not revolve around the duties, chores, and satisfactions of family life.

Many inmates live in prison like they are on a very long bad vacation, running low on cash, and stuck in a cheap motel. They pass the time doing little more than eating, sleeping, working out, watching TV, and/or playing cards. Others may spend their time hustling food, or contraband (e.g., cell phones, dope, smokes, weapons, etc.). Eventually inmates learn to "do time." This means slowing down, expecting little to happen. Both inmates and correctional officers are known to say "You've got nothing coming." This means that no one owes you anything. Slow motion is safer. Move fast, expect too much, and you get hurt.

## Prisonization

After many years in the penitentiary you become institutionalized, a process called *prisonization*. Prison is a small world, one in which people are warehoused, monitored by guards and video cameras, confined by razor wire, and guarded by gun towers. Prisoners have lived in a society built of cement and steel and share a worldview predicated on their experience of incarceration. They are tentative and insecure, for they know that society is not as free as they may once have believed, and that indeed sometimes they've been made to pay for crimes they'd previously felt assured they could commit with impunity.

By day you wait for the controlled movement that once an hour allows passage from one area of the prison to another. By night you sleep in an 8-by-10-foot cell, double-bunked with someone you'd rather not know. All the time you are subject to the orders of correctional officers and the chaos and noise of hundreds of voices reverberating off steel and concrete walls.

A convict with a number, locked up to protect the public, you live day to day where there is no place to hide from the enemies you make inside. Unfortunately, this leaves you little time to gather accurate information about the challenges that wait beyond the bars.

## Getting Out of Prison Stories

We routinely hear stories about how difficult it was for ex-convicts to readjust to life beyond bars. They couldn't find a job, afford a place to live, or get along with their parole officer (PO). A lot of people who were able to live straight and sober while they were locked up turn to drugs and alcohol almost as soon as they hit the streets.

Getting out of the joint, most men and women are disoriented, and some are even afraid. Most have "get out of prison" stories about how they'd forgotten how to time the flow of pedestrians on the sidewalk or traffic on the street and had experienced great difficulty simply walking around town. Others who've spent a considerable period of time behind bars become disoriented with new technologies, such as driving late-model cars. Even being unable to find the high-beam dimmer switch may trigger a crisis of confidence.

We know one prisoner who had just been released and was riding a Greyhound bus to the halfway house to serve out the final three months of his sentence. Shortly after settling comfortably into his seat, he had the urge to smoke a cigarette. Despite all the no smoking signs, he walked back to the restroom to have his smoke.

After the smoke detector sounded, the driver pulled the bus over on the shoulder of the Interstate. He ordered the guy out of the restroom, and warned him that it was against the law to smoke on a public bus. The ex-convict, shrugging his shoulders, returned to his seat. An hour later, he snuck back to the restroom, disabled the smoke alarm, and proceeded to light up. The driver, in his rearview mirror, saw the passenger exit the restroom and noticed smoke drifting to the ceiling. The ex-convict returned to his seat.

When the bus pulled into the station, the police were waiting for him. The bus driver had radioed ahead. When the ex-convict was questioned about his clothing and the cardboard box, he told the police that he just got out of prison. They threw him in the squad car and escorted him back to prison.

Upon his return to the penitentiary, his cell mates asked him why he came back so quickly. He foolishly related the bus story to all his buddies. The convicts were so embarrassed by his actions that they beat him up. He ended up serving the remainder of his time in protective custody (i.e., in the hole). The guys might have understood if he had been busted for illegal use of drugs or alcohol. But returning to prison for smoking a cigarette was more than they could accept.

# Getting Ready for Release

Ideally, you should begin preparing for release from prison the day you enter a correctional institution. Use your jail and prison time wisely: see incarceration as a sanctuary, a place to reflect upon your mistakes, rethink who you are and what you might become, and then begin again as a new and better person. This might include taking advantage of any and all appropriate individual and group programs. For example, nearly all prisons provide opportunities to complete adult basic education (ABE, which is eighth grade) and high school equivalency diplomas (GED/HSED—also known as twelfth grade).

Some correctional facilities offer occasional vocational and college courses. Generally, prison staff manage educational, vocational, and drug treatment programs. Volunteers or contract employees organize Alcohol or Narcotics Anonymous meetings, Bible reading, Toastmasters, or classes on anger management, family and parenting issues, or life skills.

Most prisons have two libraries, a general one filled with paperback books, and a law library required by federal law. The libraries are often the quietest and safest places in the facility. This is where you may find inmates with college degrees who might be good people to know. They can suggest better books for you to read, especially ones that might inspire you to expand your worldview.

## Making Post-Prison Plans

Unless you were sentenced to death or life without parole, sooner or later you are going to get out of the joint. All prisoners fantasize about what they will do when they return home. They dream about wild sex, eating at fancy restaurants, wearing sharp clothing, and walking beneath the stars at night.

It's time for a reality check. You might as well come to terms now with what life on the outside is really going to be like, rather than be disappointed once you're out.

The cards are stacked against you. If you are not careful, you will be violated at the halfway house or in the first year of parole and returned to jail or prison against your will.

This is why you need to carefully construct a post-release plan that anticipates the problems you are going to face. Most modern prison systems have an official form on which inmates specify where they intend to live and work or go to school. Prison case managers usually add this to inmate files. You may also want to develop a more detailed informal plan, including "things to do," and "things not to do." It goes without saying: you probably do not want to share this informal plan with prison staff. The less they know about your personal plans the better.

## Time for a Reality Check

You've been locked up a long time and have forgotten how to live in the real world. You need to remember that your life may not have been so wonderful before you entered prison. Now, as you leave the correctional facility older and hopefully a little wiser, you might be returning to the same problems you left behind.

Take a long look in the mirror (if you can find one in the joint). Will you really be welcomed back when you return home? Will your family and friends be ready to see you? What exactly has happened while you were gone?

In prison, you lived in a convict culture where everyday life is dictated by the unique environment.

Returning home, there are many little worlds; some may overlap, but each has different cultural expectations. A few steps to your left you are back with the dopers and the folks you left at the bar. Turn right and you are going to church with the bible thumpers. Get up early in the morning and you might find yourself hanging out with folks who have a work ethic. If you stay out late and go to the nightclubs, you might get caught up with the party people and hustlers. In some ways, prison was easier. You had fewer choices to make. In the free world you are free to make a lot of mistakes. But you can't afford to.

## The Art of Small Talk

Even the simple act of engaging in a conversation can be daunting for someone just released from prison. Many male ex-convicts have forgotten how to converse with women and children. They might be afraid to engage in casual talk with people they don't know well. Women prisoners might be frightened of all men.

Convicts don't do small talk well; it's hard for them to converse about the weather, the latest movie, or what was on the evening news. They do not begin conversations with polite questions like: How are you? How are you doing? How is your family? In prison, they were forced to conform to different customs.

While you are behind bars, preparing to get out, you need opportunities to practice the art of small talk. You can do this in the visiting room or on the phone with family and friends. Another approach is to take every opportunity to initiate conversations with volunteers who manage groups and events at the prison (i.e., Alcoholics Anonymous, etc.). This provides you with a chance to polish your conversational skills with someone who is in the free world.

Once you have mastered the art of casual conversation, you will find it easier to make new friends. The safest way to conduct a conversation is to ask polite questions. Most people like to talk about themselves.

In addition, be careful about whom you tell that you are an ex-convict. The general rule is not to share this information with someone you have just met, because they probably don't want or care to know. Whatever you do, don't preface your sentences by saying things like, "When I was in the joint ..." Instead, talk about neutral subjects like the weather, sports, or movies.

## So Why Do They Call It Reentry?

*Reentry* is the new term for inmates getting out of prison and returning to the community. Some prisoners have completed their sentences behind bars. This is called *mandatory release* or *expiration of sentence*. Others will have additional time to serve on parole, or what is often called *community supervision*.

In big cities and small towns all over America, police and parole officials have organized community forums where they invite local people to discuss their concerns with reentry. Law enforcement officials warn those in attendance about the "savages at the gate," the criminals getting out of prison. The Police Chief (and perhaps even the head of Probation and Parole) might incite the nebulous fear felt by many that "we" need to be better ready for "them," or else. This means hiring more police, arming them with better weapons, spending more on training, buying more squad cars, and building a new addition on the city jail. This seems to be the only solution to the bad guys who will soon be coming home.

At the same meeting, city bureaucrats will complain that there are too many people getting out of jails and prisons all at once, coming home to their communities. They express their concerns about not having enough personnel and resources to protect the community. Elected and appointed officials might think these men and women getting out of prison are the embodiment of a new crime wave that is about to explode on the scene and terrorize their once-peaceful neighborhoods.

All of this fear talk is meant to scare the good citizens so they won't mind when their property, sales, and personal income taxes rise. All those new police expenditures add up. It costs approximately $100,000 a year to hire one new police officer, with new patrol car, benefits, and pension. This doesn't even include weapons, radios, computers, uniforms, and additional training.

Sometimes citizens appear at these community forums to challenge the obvious fear tactics. People from the faith-based community, informed and experienced corrections workers, and even an ex-convict or two might attend. They might speak up and share what they know about prisoners coming home. After all, common sense tells you these people served their sentences as ordered, and now have a right to rejoin the community. Besides, maybe the community would be better served if it found the courage to develop meaningful employment and housing programs and counseling and mentoring agencies, and made a serious effort to give these correctional clients a second chance—a fair opportunity to do good.

Remember that today there are more than seven million Americans in correctional custody. If all of these people were forced to serve their entire sentence, our local, state, and federal governments would go bankrupt in no time. Without probation and parole, the criminal justice system would have to build three times as many jails and prisons—maybe one right across the street from your kids' school or your home.

So what is reentry? In reality it depends on your point of view. From the prisoners' perspective it means returning home, trying the best they can to become part of the community. Walking out of prison to return home is like Rip Van Winkle waking up after many years asleep.

If you are going back to a big city, you are simply one of many. City life can be nearly anonymous, where people might not know who their next-door neighbor is. You return to an area where the pace is so fast and everybody is in such a hurry that few people will care about who you are and where you have been for the past few months or years. The good news is that most cities have some social services for people down on their luck, and if you get desperate, you will be able to find a warm bed and a decent meal through a homeless shelter, church, or social services agency. Besides, the police are so busy with real crime, they may not have time to bother you.

The downside is that you have been living in prison where the pace is slow, and nobody is in a hurry. When you return home to a big city, you will find it difficult to catch up, compete for jobs, and afford the higher cost of living. Like a lot of ex-convicts, you might be forced to rent an inexpensive room, or take an apartment in a ghetto neighborhood, where crime is all around you.

Returning to a small town is an entirely different experience. It will seem that *everyone* knows you're an ex-convict, and they aren't going to be happy to have you around. They may even meet you at the bus station or stop by your parents' house to "welcome" you home. Meanwhile, you need to worry about a place to sleep and a way to make some money.

## Getting a Taste of Reentry

Back in the 1970s and 1980s, prisoners could qualify for pre-release programs that might have included furloughs, work release, educational release, and halfway houses. A furlough was when you temporarily got out of prison for 24 hours, three days, or maybe even a week for some special purpose. Educational release was when a prisoner serving time in a low-security institution left the facility every day to attend community college or university. Some work release programs still exist for minimum-security inmates.

### Furloughs

Unfortunately, most prison systems no longer offer furloughs, and even when they do, it's difficult to qualify for them. Too bad, because furloughs are a great way for convicts to readjust to the outside. It affords the inmate an opportunity to test out her plans for release, including finding an appropriate place to live and work. A few prison systems still authorize selected minimum-security inmates who are within one year of release to go home for a few days to see family. If your correctional facility offers this kind of program, try to take advantage of it.

Some prison systems also allow wealthy prisoners to go on a home furlough to see a parent on his or her death bed or to attend their parent's funeral. Of course, upon return the inmate will be transported in a prison van, wear restraints, and have a bill for the correctional officers' overtime pay.

Occasionally, low-security convicts may also qualify for furloughs to get critical medical attention, participate in religious instruction or services, or even speak on a college campus, if escorted by guards. Some minimum-security facilities may still allow for "unescorted furlough transfers" from one camp to another. In all these cases, the prisoners are trusted because of their good conduct record in prison, and the fact that they are nearing the completion of their sentence.

## Educational Release

Occasionally, prison systems that are relatively close to colleges and universities allow model prisoners to leave minimum-security institutions to attend the local community college or university. It's up to the inmate to pay for his or her tuition and books.

These special programs are very limited, but when they exist, they provide a few seriously motivated prisoners the opportunity to pursue higher education. Of course, if the inmate enrolls in classes, pays tuition, and then gets a "shot" or "ticket" (a disciplinary report that typically gets a prisoner time in the hole), he or she won't be going to class again anytime soon.

## Work Release Center

A work release center is a minimum-security facility operated by the Department of Corrections (DOC). The building may have a security fence with restricted entry and exit. At these facilities, inmate movement is monitored closely, and the doors and windows are locked at all times. There are different housing units with gradations of privilege to be earned by prisoners.

For example, after many years of incarceration, you might be transferred to a DOC Work Release Center to serve out the last year of your sentence. You'll probably spend the first 90 days in orientation, evaluation, and training to look for a job. Then you'll be released for eight hours during the day to work at a job in the community. If you are unable to secure employment or you get fired, you may be returned to prison. Prisoners can catch disciplinary violations and be returned to a penitentiary or correctional institution for refusing the first available menial job or for failing to return promptly to the work release center. Predictably, there is high rate of failure in these programs. We discuss halfway houses and work release centers in more detail in Chapter 4.

### Halfway House

A halfway house is a generic term for any facility operated by a government or nonprofit agency, where prisoners will live for a few months upon leaving prison. All these programs have their situational advantages and disadvantages. We discuss these in greater detail in the next chapter.

## Reentry for Joe and Jill

Both Joe and Jill Convict were sentenced to 10 years in prison, followed by a second 10 years to be served on "community supervision."

Joe Convict came to prison at age 20. After a decade of being incarcerated, he is now 30 years old. He completed his GED and a few college courses that were offered by a local community college. More important, Joe is an avid reader. As a prisoner, he visited the general library every week to search for serious nonfiction. He has read the entire library selection of "how to" books on health, finance, relationships, and marriage. Occasionally, he found a college textbook; it made little difference if it was biology or history.

He read it to improve his vocabulary, increase his analytical skills, and prepare for college. He avoided the law library, as he knew his case was helpless and he had no chance of appeal. Besides, the so-called "jail-house lawyers" drew heat and spent too much time in the "hole." Joe passed as much time as possible sitting quietly on his bunk reading the best books he could find.

Jill convict came to prison in her late 20s, after collecting numerous and assorted misdemeanors. She is a single mother with a number of children conceived with various boyfriends. She is also a high school dropout. Jill was sexually abused as a child, dropped out of school, ran away from home, and got involved with alcohol and illegal drugs. Ever since then, Jill has been in and out of jail serving short sentences for relatively minor offences. After many years of shoplifting, passing bad checks, and using hard drugs, she was finally charged and convicted of a felony and sent to prison. Like a lot of women prisoners she thinks a lot about getting out and retrieving her children. She hopes to complete her formal education, get some job skills, and prepare for a better job. Most important, she needs to stay clean and keep a job so that she can support her kids.

Although many things are the same for both men and women who leave jail and prison, there are special circumstances for ex-connets, as female prisoners are often called. This is especially true if their children have been taken away from them by social services or if they are in the custody of their relatives and/or abusive husbands.

# Chapter 2

## Free at Last?

Most correctional facilities have an official pre-release program. Inmates nearing their release date are called to a meeting that may last an hour or two. One of the prison administrators presides and invites one or two parole officers (POs) and some volunteers from the community to come out to the prison to talk to the convicts.

Typically, a PO stands up and tells you what the rules of parole are and how important it is to abide by them. Somebody from the state job agency talks about the steps to take when looking for a job and describes the resources they have in their office. A retired corporate executive, maybe a former banker, gives a speech about budgeting your money, how to open a checking account, and the need to set aside savings. Finally, a social service worker talks about where you might find some assistance, like food stamps or an emergency shelter.

The scene resembles an inner-city high school classroom. The room is filled with convicts slouched in their chairs. A few people might ask questions, but nobody takes notes. Most of the inmates appear bored and uninterested in what the speakers have to say.

Joe looks around the room and realizes that many of these guys have been through pre-release before. The PO is not going to be their officer. They are never going to see these individual social service workers and do-gooders again when they walk out the door. At the end of the meeting, the inmates are not particularly enlightened or inspired. They don't really think that the speakers care much about their success. They already know what they want to do once they are released, and it has little to do with the pep talk.

## Joe's Last Day in Prison

Joe has been waiting for this day for 10 long years. At 6 A.M. the cell house bell rings. Five hundred convicts open their eyes to another day just like the last one. But for Joe this is the day he is finally going home. He showers and dresses in the same khaki prison uniform, but this morning he will not go to the chow hall for breakfast and then to work in one of the penitentiary factories or shops. Instead, he empties his locker and throws everything in a cardboard box.

His fellow inmates have all gone to breakfast. He sits on his bed in the empty cell block, and he is scared to death. Staring at the dirty concrete wall, Joe notices that he has not packed his calendar. It's still glued to the wall. He reaches up and tears it down, and throws it into the garbage.

He is waiting for the "call out" and the correctional officer who will escort him on the "Merry Go Round," the process of going from department to department to clear his accounts and get the appropriate official signatures. But Joe doesn't want to walk through the prison. He doesn't want somebody to start a fight with him. This morning, he doesn't want to take any chances. He will skip breakfast and stay in his cell. That cell became his home and sanctuary from all the penitentiary madness and violence.

Over the past few days, Joe has said goodbye to his close friends. He gave away his extra clothes, legal pads, and books. As the men wander down the range on their way to breakfast, a few of his cell house buddies stop to wish him good luck, shake his hand, or give him a hug. Some of them he will miss; others he won't. Joe knows most of the inmates will make it out eventually, but a few will die inside.

Finally, Joe hears his name and number called out over the barely audible speaker system, "Joe Convict number 24456-071, report to the officer's station." Joe walks to the front of the cell house, where he gives his name to the officer sitting at a desk inside a small office. The CO says, "Joe, this is Officer Jones; he will escort you on your Merry-Go-Round." As the cell house door is unlocked, Officer Jones steps back and waits for Joe to walk ahead. Even on his last day, Joe must follow prison protocol by walking in front of the correctional officer so the CO can keep a close eye on him, and bark orders as needed.

## A Ride on the Merry-Go-Round

Merry-Go-Round is the official name for the process where an inmate checks out of a federal prison. The same activity goes by different names in various state correctional systems.

Joe makes his way down the corridor through more security hubs and sally ports to reach the property room. He carries his official Merry-Go-Round Memo, which lists each prison location he must visit to have correctional workers sign, date, and record the time.

The Property Room Inmate Clerk looks at the memo and retrieves Joe's personal effects, which he surrendered a decade ago. Joe opens the package to find his battered old wallet. Predictably, his cash and credit cards disappeared years ago, along with his wedding ring and watch. Standing at the counter, with one correctional officer behind him and another in front, he knows there's no point in mentioning the missing items. At least the wallet still contains a few family photos and his expired driver's license. Joe signs for his belongings and, without a word, turns toward the door.

The next stop is the "Store," where Joe will be dressed out in cheap street clothes. He is told to strip down to his underwear and to deposit his prison khakis in a nearby laundry basket. The prison will wash and issue his clothes to another inmate. A guard gives him a new civilian shirt, pair of pants, and socks and shoes. He puts them on even though they don't fit well. Then he asks for a coat. The officer points to a rack of inexpensive cotton jackets. Joe tries one on and it fits.

Sadly, he is almost grateful for his new outfit, for he has heard that many men walk out of jail or prison wearing convict uniforms, orange jumpsuits, or prison blues, their prison numbers still sewn on their shirts or DOC written on the back. It's a wonder that they do not get shot by the police, who think they are escapees. Joe will be okay, though—he has a new coat that at least will cover his tattooed arms.

The first thing most guys do when they get out of the joint is dump their cheap rags in the garbage or burn them in the back yard as a symbolic gesture to celebrate their freedom.

Joe's ride on the Merry-Go-Round continues as the CO escorts him to the library, education wing, prison factory, infirmary, and commissary to review his accounts, to the business office to sign papers to forward his commissary money to the halfway house, and then finally to the administration building to stand in line at his case manager's door. Hopefully, his case manager will have his release, travel, and halfway house papers completed. Joe is being transferred from "the big house" (the prison) to "the small house" (a community halfway house). The case manager will send him on his way with his release papers, a bus ticket, and maybe even some "gate money"—a few dollars so he can buy a meal on his way to the halfway house.

Remember, in most prisons inmates cannot possess coin or paper money. Instead, the postal money orders that Joe received in the mail from home, or money earned as "inmate pay" working in the prison factory or other institutional jobs is deposited by the facility directly into his commissary account. While he was in the penitentiary, he had an inmate ID card that was used at the commissary and with vending machines. That money will now be transferred by the prison to his new account at the halfway house, which may take weeks to arrive. When Joe walks out the prison gate, the only money he might have is the "gate money" he receives from the case manager. If he is lucky he will receive $10 to $50 the day he leaves. Some correctional institutions give no gate money at all.

## Joe Is Going Home

It's now noon, and Joe sits nervously on a bench waiting for the officers to escort him to the prison gate. He is so excited he can hardly sit still. His "get out of jail" paperwork is inside his coat pocket, and he has a broad smile on his face. On his lap he clutches the cardboard box, his name and prison number written in magic marker on one side.

Finally, an officer strolls up, asks to look at his paperwork, and tells him to stand up and walk to the front gate. The CO then picks up the telephone and looks high above the wall and waves to another officer in the gun tower. Joe hears a loud buzz as the heavy metal door is unlocked. He stands in front of the door, and the officer pushes it open and instructs Joe to step out. The officer looks at Joe intently and says, "Good luck and don't come back."

Joe takes a big breath and steps forward. He is now outside the prison walls. With his arms wrapped around the cardboard box, he walks down the sidewalk to the curb. Joe puts the box down and, for the first time in many years, takes in the unobstructed expanse of green and blue that stretches to the horizon. It's overwhelming. He has gone from the little world to the big world. An hour later a taxi arrives to take him to the truck stop where he will catch the Greyhound bus. Joe is going home.

## Jill's Time in Prison Was Different

Jill had a slightly different experience in prison, including the day she got out. Her facility, the only women's prison in the state—a combination minimum-, medium-, and maximum-security institution—has no gun towers or outside walls. Instead, it is surrounded by a chain-link perimeter fence with one small roll of razor wire, and a few strands of barbed wire at the top. Women prisoners attempt very few escapes.

Jill did 10 years after a string of convictions for relatively minor felonies. She was housed most of the time in a dormitory. She went through the Merry-Go-Round process this morning, packed up her box, and donned new clothes her family sent her in preparation for this day. Walking out of the dormitory, there were a lot of hugs, kisses, and crying as she said goodbye to the other "ladies."

In prison, women often create pseudo families, with different inmates taking on roles as father, mother, and daughters. Jill came to prison as a "daughter," although she has become something of a mother figure to several of the new inmates. Today she is surrounded by her "daughters," who are distraught about their "mom" leaving.

Her conditions of confinement were significantly different than Joe's. At least she could see the green of the farm fields and distant horizon through the lighter-security chain-link fence. In a women's prison, there is also much less violence. Although there are fights and arguments almost daily, they don't amount to much.

Nevertheless, women do suffer in prison, in some ways more than the men. They seem to deteriorate faster, maybe from the stress, humiliation, or worry about their children. As the years pass, they may become self-destructive. This may explain why suicide is more common in women's prisons.

Because "connets" are not treated as harshly as men in prison, they may not take release as seriously as men do. They tend to think the system will forgive them if they break the rules of parole. After all, chances are they smiled and winked their way through a lot of problems in the past. Some of these women think they can use their charm to "get over" on male halfway house staff and POs, too.

The correctional officers handcuff and shackle her before she steps into the unmarked black DOC van. Although Jill would have preferred being picked up by her mother, she is still technically in the custody of the DOC.

Most of the women will be driven to halfway houses, but Jill is doing mandatory release (MR), meaning that she has completed her entire prison sentence and thus has no halfway house assignment; however, she still has additional time to do on community supervision. It's early morning when the DOC vehicle drives her directly home to her parents. As she gets out of the van, she is greeted by her mother, who waits for her on the front porch. Her mother looks older than the last time Jill saw her. The wrinkles are deeper in her face. Jill hugs her mom, and after a minute or two, asks to see her dad, who waits for her inside.

That afternoon, her mom takes her to school to pick up the kids. This is the first time in many years the children have seen their mother dressed in civilian clothes. Jill can't help but marvel at how fast they have grown up while she was away. Jill is finally home.

## Halfway Free

Many convicts released from correctional institutions are assigned to halfway houses. After they complete their time at the halfway house, they are placed on parole. Others simply walk out the door on "Mandatory Release" or "Expiration of Sentence." Generally, only minimum- or medium-security prisoners receive halfway house assignment at the end of their prison sentence. Halfway house assignments are typically 30 to 180 days, depending upon the prison system, beds available, and what is politically fashionable in the jurisdiction.

Most hard-core maximum-security inmates do all their time in the high-security or super-max penitentiary and then go straight to the streets. The system doesn't trust them to adjust and conform to halfway house rules and regulations.

Joe is an exception, because although he is being released from a maximum-security penitentiary, he has a good conduct record, with no loss of "good time" (i.e., time off your sentence for not breaking the rules). He is being transferred to a halfway house on the favorable recommendation of his prison case manager.

Jill was not given an opportunity to complete her sentence at a halfway house. Instead, she was forced to do her entire sentence in prison. Many states do not have enough halfway houses for the growing number of women prisoners being released.

Convicts released from the penitentiary go through a euphoric stage when they rediscover free time, open space, and new possibilities. Unfortunately, this initial infatuation with freedom is frequently short-lived.

# Chapter 3

## Probation and Parole

Even before Joe and Jill exit prison, they know that in short order they will be required to report to a parole office. They don't expect to find a friend or mentor at the office. They don't want to go there and do not look forward to being supervised by another government agent. But you never know—they might get lucky and end up being assigned a decent parole officer (PO).

Joe will first go to the halfway house. After a few months there, his PO will come to the halfway house to meet with him. Because Jill is going straight home to her parents, she won't need to go to a halfway house. Instead, she will have to report to the parole office within 48 hours of her release.

We want you to know how to survive reentry, avoid parole revocation, not catch a new case, and never return to jail or prison. Your struggle will not be easy, as there are many obstacles to overcome. In some ways, the biggest fight may be with your own capacity or determination for self-destruction. Just remember: when the prison doors open, you are not free.

## Probation

The vast majority of criminal charges are misdemeanors, which are criminal convictions with sentences of a year or less. Misdemeanors are typically punishable by a fine, community service, less than a year in jail, a year or less on probation, or some combination of these sanctions. In comparison, a felony conviction carries a sentence that is longer than a year and a day behind bars.

When a judge hands down a felony sentence, she can order prison or probation. Probation is a suspended sentence, whereby if the person violates the conditions of probation he will then spend the balance of the sentence in jail or prison. In many respects probation is a gift given by the judge to the person convicted of a crime. As long as the probationer behaves himself, obeys the rules of probation, and does what he is told, he will not do more jail or prison time.

A suspended sentence could be for anywhere from 1 year to 50 or more years, depending on the crime. For example, a person could get 10 years probation for large-scale embezzlement from a bank. The judge might hand down a suspended sentence if he wants the convicted person to make restitution, which means paying back the bank. If the convict goes to prison, she will not be able to work to pay the restitution. The financial institution might even ask the judge to give her probation so they can recoup the loss. Another example might be a senior citizen convicted of child molestation, who might get probation for the rest of his life.

Approximately two thirds of all criminal convictions result in probation. Typically, first-time nonviolent offenders will be sentenced to probation. Defendants given probation must report on a regular basis to their probation officer and/or submit to random drug testing. They must avoid "catching another case" (e.g., being arrested, charged, and/or convicted of another crime). As a condition of their probation, they must work a legitimate job, attend school, and/or demonstrate that they are actively looking for work. Both probationers and parolees must also abide by many rules that we discuss later in the book.

Many people fail probation, either as a result of their failure to abide by the rules or circumstances beyond their control. When they fail, they are arrested, handcuffed, taken to jail, and processed back into the correctional system. A formal hearing will determine their ultimate fate. If they were originally convicted of a felony and sentenced to many years, they will be transported from jail to prison to complete the sentence.

## The Origins of Probation

Probation has a long and colorful history in Europe and America It began when selected people convicted of crimes were "referred to clergy," where priests and ministers would attend to their "supervision and salvation." Eventually, governments replaced the clergy with full-time paid officials.

In the United States, probation had its roots in the 1800s with John Augustus, a shoemaker who took care of drunks who were in and out of jail. He was able to keep them on the straight and narrow so they would not be recommitted. Augustus' work with drunks impressed the political elites of Boston so much that they convinced the local government to legitimize his position. Later, the State of Massachusetts passed the first probation act creating a probation agency first in Boston, then in other parts of the state. Other jurisdictions around the country, seeing the success in Massachusetts, followed suit.

## Many People Don't Realize They Are Convicted Felons

We estimate that millions of Americans are convicted felons and don't even know it. Many people don't understand the difference between a misdemeanor and a felony, they didn't care at the time, and/or nobody ever explained it to them.

A felony is any crime that carries a sentence of more than one year. There are major felonies like homicide and bank robbery, and minor felonies like possession of small quantities of illegal substances or failure to cover a bounced check. The criminal justice system converts misdemeanors to felonies by simply increasing the jail or prison time a particular offense may carry. Over the years there has been a steady "felonization" of criminal offenses.

Many people are arrested for some relatively minor event and then charged with a series of offenses, some of them misdemeanors and others felonies. Eventually they plea bargain, meaning that one or more charges are dropped in exchange for a plea of guilt or "no contest" to one or more other charges. In the process, the defendants may think the felonies were dropped, as they were only given probation.

For example, at the point of arrest, if the person has valid identification and no previous criminal record, she might simply be issued a citation or court summons. She will not even know that she has committed a felony.

It is not unusual for a person to never wear handcuffs or spend time in a jail cell, and then plead to a felony and receive probation. He may even get "nonreport probation," where he is not required to report to a probation office. So, because he was not taken to the police station or placed in a jail cell, he assumes he could not possibly be a felon.

This is common in small-scale drug-possession cases in big cities. This may have happened to you when you were a college student or young adult living in a large metropolitan area. Assuming people are polite, the arresting officers might confiscate the dope, verify the defendants' identification, and simply let them go. The police call this "catch and release," like returning small fish to a river or lake.

The defendants might not even have been required to appear in court. They simply hired an attorney who plea bargained for them. A judge handed down a conviction that required the offender to maybe pay a fine, or do community service, and then serve a suspended sentence of more than one year on nonreport probation. All they had to do was stay out of trouble and avoid being arrested again.

Years later, they don't remember what happened because it was so long ago, or they were in a marijuana-induced daze at the time. Because the person lived in a state where felons could vote, he had no interest in buying a firearm, and he owned his own business or worked in jobs that didn't involve a personal background check, he was able to live his life without ever being identified as a felon. It never occurred to him that he was a felon.

If his conviction happened in the 1960s, 1970s, or 1980s, he is probably home free. If his sentence was in the 1990s, after most jurisdictions' criminal justice records were computerized, it still may catch up with him the next time he applies for a job, gets arrested, or gets his name in the newspaper.

Finally, we suspect that a lot of middle-class adults would like to forget some of the trouble they got into when they were young and wild. Maybe they got busted for "unauthorized use of a motor vehicle" or "criminal damage to property" and just want to bury the memory. They know they have an old felony conviction, but never discuss it.

## Who Do You Report To?

Probation and parole officers typically work out of the same office. Probation officers handle the lightweight cases, usually juveniles and young adults convicted of minor offenses. Parole officers usually handle the heavyweights, the convicted felons who often went to prison and who are returning home after a long stretch in the pen. Probation and parole officers are both known as POs.

If you are granted probation, you will be reporting to a county, state, or federal parole office. If you get federal probation, you probably will not report every month as the feds are too busy supervising parolees who just got out of Federal Correctional Institutions and United States Penitentiaries. In general, the federal government uses probation less than most state court systems. This is because federal courts tend to hand down stiffer sentences.

In contrast, by law most state governments must balance their annual budgets, which causes them to be a bit more restrained when it comes to spending millions of dollars on new correctional facilities. So, when the prisons are over capacity, state courts are more inclined to sentence convicted defendants to probation.

In most states, juveniles or young adults are the most likely to be ordered to actually report to a probation office on a regular basis. If you are a more responsible older adult, you may only have to report for a few months or not at all. It depends on your jurisdiction, your age, your demeanor, your prior record, and the disposition of your case.

If you are ordered to report to the Division of Probation and Parole office, do it. If you fail to show up, your probation or parole will be revoked (it might even result in a new charge) and you will be picked up by law enforcement officers and taken directly to the local jail.

## What to Expect

When you go to your first appointment with your parole or probation officer, dress like you are on a job interview. But don't be surprised by how others dress and behave as they wait for their meetings.

You might be waiting along with 100 other people—some of them quite dangerous-looking—in a crowded, dingy reception area. So be calm and be patient. Don't schedule a critical appointment such as a job interview, a visit to the doctor, or a hot date after your probation meeting, and plan to spend at least three hours waiting.

Don't constantly ask the secretary when you are going to see your probation officer. And don't ask anybody for any favors. When you enter that office, you are treated like you are a nobody; and as we've said before, you've got nothing coming. They are going to make you do the time one way or another. Just slow down and do what they tell you to do.

## Things to Avoid

As you are subject to testing for drugs and alcohol, avoid these substances at all costs. In addition, do not carry anything that could be considered as a possible weapon. This includes nail files, pocket knives, pepper spray, mace, or, God forbid, a machete. Even if you are a mechanic, leave the screwdriver in the shop.

Upon entering the building, you may have to walk through a metal detector and be asked to dump the contents of your purse, backpack, or briefcase on a table for inspection.

The security guards or POs may also order you to stand with your hands on the wall and spread your legs while they frisk you and go through your pockets. If they don't trust you or you are giving them lip, they may even ask you to strip so they can thoroughly search everything you are wearing. POs are by their nature very suspicious.

Our best advice here is to leave everything possible in your car or at home. Only bring your identification when you enter the building. Leave your wallet and/or purse in your car. The officer can search them and record any information they find, including the telephone numbers and addresses they find from the business cards and scraps of paper you have accumulated.

If you owe the court any money, they can even take the cash they find in your wallet, purse, or pocket. Don't ever bring a checkbook into their office, as they might check your balance and demand that you write them a check on the spot.

If you were silly enough to bring in your cash or checkbook and they make you pay, at the very least, make sure you get a receipt.

Finally, leave all legally prescribed medications in your car. Let's say you have a prescription for Oxycodine. If they find the pills on you, they may accuse you of stealing or selling drugs.

No matter what happens, don't argue with the PO. If you get out of line he may handcuff you, and the next thing you know you will be off to jail or prison again.

## Pee Testing

Most probationers and parolees are required to have their urine tested for alcohol or drugs. Typically, you are required to pee in a cup in front of an officer. This prevents you from slipping in your younger brother's clean urine that you collected from him at home earlier that morning. They can test you anytime they want—when you visit the office or when they make a home or work visit.

Over the past two decades, an entire industry has cropped up that sells "clean" urine to people who use drugs or alcohol and don't want it to be detected. There are also a number of herbal-drug detection-busting concoctions on the market. These items try to either mask or dilute your urine so you can fly under the radar. Some drug test survivors say simply drinking lots of water to flush your system is the best thing to do.

Then again, we have heard tales of persons who smoke pot every day and never get busted during a pee test. How could this be? Maybe the parole office used a drug screen protocol that did not test for marijuana. Instead, their urine was tested for more serious drugs. Or perhaps the parole office that collected the samples only had a small percentage of them tested.

Unless you want to play Russian roulette with the pee testers, perhaps this is a good time to simply clean up your act for at least the duration of your parole. It is also a good time to think about attending Alcoholics or Narcotics Anonymous meetings.

# The Day-to-Day Reality of Probation and Parole

In the past few decades, the use of community corrections has ebbed and flowed based on public perceptions and government funding. Many studies have been done on the effectiveness of community correction. In general, the results suggest that although probation and parole have minimal effect on recidivism, they significantly reduce the costs of incarceration.

Beginning in the 1970s, many constituencies were fed up with what they perceived were the failures of community corrections. There was a growing perception that the criminal justice system needed to get tougher on crime.

During the 1980s, states and the federal government started experimenting with, and then implementing, new kinds of sanctions. These included intensive probation and parole supervision, home arrest, electronic monitoring, and chemical castration.

## Intensive Probation and Parole

The national media has done a pretty good job of terrorizing the public with stories about people on probation or parole committing serious crimes. Eventually, the average citizen began to think that probation and parole were too easy, simply a slap on the wrist. This led state and federal parole offices to implement new programs such as "Intensive Probation or Parole," where men and women who were perceived to be more dangerous were kept on a shorter leash. Probation and parole clients on intensive probation are ordered to report once a day or once a week. They are also subject to "home visits" and regular searches by parole authorities.

## House Arrest

Another innovation was the imposition of "house arrest." This means you are restricted from leaving your home between certain hours. For example, the probationer or parolee is usually allowed out during the day to go to work or school. A person might have a "night curfew," where she must be home between 9 P.M. and 6 A.M. This sanction is frequently used for sex offenders and juveniles.

## Going High Tech

The use of so-called "techno-corrections" is the latest innovation in community corrections. This includes electronic monitoring and the use of drugs.

Electronic monitoring (EM) is used to track your whereabouts. EM consists of a wireless electronic device that officials can use to monitor your movements. The device is attached to a heavy plastic strap that is fastened on your ankle. The new and improved models employ Global Positioning System (GPS) technology, which links up to satellites. It can be used to track you as you walk or drive across the city.

The use of EM has grown considerably, from approximately 95 individuals in Florida in 1986 to about 70,000 individuals monitored by local, state, and federal entities today. But EM is not without its difficulties. During the 1990s, reports surfaced that cited numerous problems, including substantial up-front costs, the cost of running the system effectively, "bugs" within the EM technology, and community reaction to criminals who are on EM. In short, EM has a lot of problems and is not the panacea that authorities hoped it would be.

A variant of EM is the Secure Continuous Remote Alcohol Monitor (SCRAM). This is an ankle bracelet that analyzes a person's sweat for the presence of alcohol in the bloodstream. It is increasingly being used as a condition of probation or parole in several jurisdictions in the United States. SCRAM was introduced in 2003; by summer of 2007, its manufacturers claimed that it has been used on 40,000 individuals. SCRAM has been sported by well-known American celebrities like actors Lindsay Lohan, Tracey Morgan, and Michelle Rodriguez.

## Chemical Castration

Since the mid-1990s, states including California, Georgia, Florida, Texas, and Wisconsin require men convicted of sexual offenses with minors to be chemically castrated upon release into the community. Males receive shots of Depo-Provera, a drug that lowers the body's production of testosterone and hampers the sex drive.

EM and the administration of certain medication are high-tech tools used to manage difficult populations, and they may decrease the need to personally monitor some individuals on the PO's caseload.

# Joe and Jill on Parole

In prison, Joe and Jill lived with boredom, stress, and violence. On the street, they face many other challenges, including the perils of parole. They know that community custody can be dangerous.

Almost half of all parolees get their parole status revoked and are returned to jail or prison. Most revocations are usually for technical violations and not because parolees have committed another criminal offense. Unfortunately, over the past 40 years, POs have shifted their focus from being resource brokers/social workers to law enforcement officers. In other words, they seem to care less about helping probationers and parolees succeed than they do about making sure they don't violate rules, however minor.

# Chapter 4

## Halfway Houses and
## Work Release Centers

The cab drops Joe off at the truck stop. The fare was paid by the prison. Joe decides to get a late breakfast at the truck-stop café. He takes a table at the back of the room. A waitress brings him water and a menu. Joe has forgotten what it's like to order, as he has not seen a menu in a long time. He looks up from his menu and stares at the waitress's figure and then off into the distance. Taking in his cheap coat, cardboard box, and bad haircut, the waitress realizes that Joe has just been released from the prison down the Interstate.

Just like Jake and Elwood in the movie the *Blues Brothers,* Joe would like nothing more than to go out for a big meal in a high-class French restaurant. But he should keep things simple because his digestive system won't be able to handle rich food. Besides, he needs to save what little money he has in his pocket until he gets to the city. Eventually, his folks or friends might treat him to a decent meal at a local steak house to celebrate his new freedom.

The waitress brings Joe the breakfast special, coffee, and some apple pie. Joe leans forward, with one arm on each side of the plate, and gobbles up everything in a few bites. Leaving the check on the table, he grabs a six-pack of beer from the cooler, hides it under his coat, and proceeds to the cashier counter to buy smokes. He is a bit overwhelmed by the choices, but he manages to purchase a pack of cigarettes and a lighter, and then strides to the door.

Meanwhile, the waitress returns to the table where Joe sat. She peers out the window to see him walking to his bus. Joe had forgotten to pay for the meal. The waitress has a brother in prison, and her husband is an ex-convict. She shakes her head as she tears up the check and clears the dishes.

As Joe rides the bus to the city, he stares out the windows and thinks about what could have been. He got his divorce papers two years into his 10-year sentence and he stopped getting letters from his kids more than four years ago. Still, Joe wonders what his ex-wife is doing, where the family lives, and if the kids are okay. But that will have to wait.

As the bus speeds down the freeway, Joe sits at the back while he finishes the six-pack. The Miller Lite cans roll across the floor. He can see the bus driver staring at him in his rearview mirror. Joe reaches in his pocket for his new Zippo and pack of Camel straights. He decides to cool it and wait until he gets to the city for another smoke. It would be too embarrassing to be sent back to prison for smoking a cigarette on a bus.

Upon being released from the state penitentiary, Joe has 12 hours to report to a halfway house, located in a seedy inner-city neighborhood. He gets off the bus at the downtown station and, too shy to ask for directions to the halfway house, he lifts up his jacket collar to protect himself from the cold air and starts walking down the street, hoping he is headed in the right direction.

The facility is operated by the state Department of Corrections (DOC). It's a new building with an official sign out front. Before Joe even walks in, he notices the bars on the windows. He presses the doorbell. Like most correctional facilities, the place has controlled entry and exit. A surly correctional officer opens the door and gives Joe permission to enter.

Joe walks in and gives his name, inmate number, and paperwork to a CO sitting behind a counter. The officer hands him a rule book and directs him down the hall to the dormitory where an inmate/orderly show him his bed. He will do three to six months at the halfway house, and then he will be released on parole.

## Halfway Out or Halfway In

Most men and women getting out of prison are given an assignment of one to six months in a community facility. These are usually simply called halfway houses, but they might also be referred to as residential work release centers, pre-release centers, or training centers. Regardless of their official name, they are all designed to help prisoners make the transition from prison to the community.

Despite their names and the fact that they are located off prison grounds, halfway houses are correctional institutions, just one step away from going into or getting out of prison. Many states have numerous facilities that serve as both "halfway in" and "halfway out" residential correctional facilities.

"Halfway in" refers to a person on probation or parole who has failed to comply with his court orders or needs residential services for various reasons. It may just be that his parole officer (PO) doesn't want him on the street, but also prefers not to send him to prison. The person may be ordered to live in a halfway house for an indeterminate time, which could be a few days, a number of weeks, or a few months.

"Halfway in" is usually reserved for juveniles or young adults. As part of their probation, they may serve a short sentence in a halfway house instead of going to prison. For instance, if a juvenile violates her probation by drinking beer or running away from home, the probation officer might give her another chance by ordering the offender to report to a halfway house rather than sending her directly to a juvenile detention facility. If she shows up as directed and conforms to the rules, she will avoid further incarceration.

A PO might also use a halfway house to accommodate elderly or people with medical problems he does not believe will be given appropriate care in prison. As halfway houses are located in the community, prisoners are more likely to have better access to medical services and hospitals. Sometimes an elderly man likes his booze, can't stay away from the casino, abuses prescription medication, or is developing dementia or Alzheimer's. The PO decides his client needs 24-hour supervision, so he sends him to the halfway house instead of prison.

Women may also get a second chance by being sent to a halfway house. Maybe she just got out of prison a few years back, is still on parole, and is now homeless. She could even have custody of her children but has nowhere suitable to live.

The PO doesn't want her living on the street or in a community shelter, perhaps sleeping in a room filled with men. While most homeless shelters only take men, there is a growing population of women, and even displaced families, who ask to be taken in. If a shelter doesn't accept women and families, it may give them vouchers for cheap motels or budget hotels.

Although she might not have violated any rules of parole, the PO knows she has a history of abusing alcohol and drugs, and of being abused by men. He might suggest that she move into a halfway house, where theoretically she will be safer and less likely to drift back into the dangerous activities of street life.

## Inner-City Halfway Houses

If you are assigned to a halfway house, do not expect it to be located in middle-class suburbia. If you are lucky, you will be assigned to one that is situated in an industrial or commercial section of the city close to downtown. At least there you will be close to businesses that might consider hiring ex-convicts. Maybe you will even be able to walk to work instead of taking public transportation.

Most halfway houses are in the inner city. This means a low-income neighborhood, with high unemployment and crime. These urban ghettos are home to a proliferation of community punishment services, including halfway houses, residential treatment centers, work release centers, parole offices, and substance abuse centers. As the number of prisoners, parolees, and felons grows, these communities are transformed into "felon ghettoes," populated by the victims and perpetrators of crime as well as the criminal justice system itself.

It's not unusual for an ex-convict to walk out the front door of his halfway house and be confronted by dope dealers, prostitutes, and gang bangers. At least prison provided you an opportunity to communicate with all kinds of people. Use the language skills you learned in the joint to protect yourself on the street. But do not get too familiar with the folks slinging dope or the women in miniskirts. You do not want to invite the attention of the police or be observed by halfway house staff. Best to keep your distance if you can, go about your business without getting caught up in all the action on the corner.

Street thugs are no fools. They know that prisoners who just returned to the community and are living in halfway houses are often looking for drugs and sex. They can build a new clientele by simply observing who enters and exits the halfway house, and introducing themselves to potential customers.

Avoid the fast lane at all cost, or you may return to the joint on a new charge. Your first responsibility to yourself is not to get arrested on the street, or violated at the halfway house, and returned to prison. So be careful where you venture, who you speak with, and where your curiosity takes you.

## Suburban Halfway Houses

Halfway houses in middle-class neighborhoods, as rare as they are, present a different set of problems. Remember, you have been locked up a long time, and have forgotten how to manage your reputation and presence in public. With few clothes, and less money, you probably look a bit shabby. White, black, or brown, you look pale after years in the joint where you received little sun. You have that penitentiary complexion. You walk, talk, and look like a convict once removed. Besides, your prison tattoos are showing.

So don't be surprised if middle-class folks, and other conventional types, avoid you like the plague. You would do the same thing if you were in their shoes.

Take it slow. Buy some new clothes. Try to avoid using prison slang and profanity. Make an effort to look and act like a regular Joe or Jill. As time goes by, people will start to accept you as part of the community.

## State and Federal Halfway Houses

Most halfway houses are owned and operated by state or federal governments. The Federal Bureau of Prisons (FBOP) and the many state DOCs prefer to place inmates in their own facilities, where they dictate the rules and maintain standards. They usually construct new halfway houses with built-in security features like video cameras, telephone monitoring, and electronically operated doors.

These community facilities are usually located in industrial or commercial districts and look like warehouses or small factories. Outside there might be a sign that reads "DOC Work Release Center," or "Federal Reentry Center." If there is a parking lot, it's typically small, as only the correctional staff, volunteers, and visitors are allowed to park there. Halfway house residents walk or ride the bus. The place may also have a recreational yard. The entire facility may be fenced in, usually with an 8- to 12-foot chain link.

Inside the halfway house, it looks and feels like a minimum-security prison, with 50 to 500 inmates housed inside. There is a "front desk" where one or more corrections officers sit behind a tall counter. The personnel wear the same DOC uniform as in prisons, but they are not armed. If they have problems with inmates they can't handle, they call the local police.

The personnel direct human traffic in and out of the building, pressing buttons to "buzz" inmates through the security doors. At night, the staff watch television, make their rounds, and try not to get caught sleeping on duty.

The building includes a number of small dorms where the inmates sleep. The beds and lockers are the same as in prison. Down the hall there is a large common bathroom shared by all the residents. Most halfway houses also have common rooms where residents can meet with visitors, watch television, or use computers to type up resumés, and search employment and housing databases.

## Private Contract Halfway Houses

Several nonprofit agencies, including faith-based organizations, manage halfway houses. When the prison populations increase, DOCs and the FBOP solicit more venders to provide halfway house services. Conversely, the legislature or prison administrators might decide to cut community program funding, resulting in fewer contracts with private entities. The general rule is that they try to fill their own facilities first and budget as little as possible on private halfway houses.

Community corrections has become a big business. There are many small and large private corporations competing for govern-ment contracts. They may be "for-profit," privately held companies, or publicly owned corporations including Corrections Corporation of America, which is traded on the New York Stock Exchange. Most, however, are not-for-profit agencies, many of them faith-based, meaning they are directly managed by a church or affiliated with a religion.

### Faith-Based Halfway Houses

Volunteers of America is a national, nonprofit, faith-based organi-zation that manages halfway houses and human service programs in many towns and cities all over America. We especially like this organization because they hire ex-convicts to work in their pro-grams and halfway houses.

The Salvation Army, another faith-based group, has a reputation for running excellent halfway houses for folks coming out of prison. Originating in England in the nineteenth century, the Salvation Army manages charity and social service programs all over the world. Although they are a Christian organization, they do not push religion on the people they serve.

In the United States, the Salvation Army likes to buy up old motels and hotels and convert them into shelters for homeless families. They provide free rooms and meals for these families while they seek employment and attempt to get themselves back on their feet again. They contract with state and federal prison systems to accept halfway house inmates in their shelters for homeless people. The per diem the state and federal authorities pay for each prisoner helps to support the cost of owning and running the shelter.

The inmates are usually housed two to a room. The accommodations are known to be the best in the business, much better than the standard DOC facilities. The best news is that the Salvation Army personnel pretty much leave you alone, allow you to come and go as you please, do not usually require drug or alcohol testing, and have a soup kitchen or free pantry on the premises.

Dismas House, operated by Catholic Charities, also operates halfway houses all over the country. Many of these are in abandoned churches that have been remodeled, with rows of rooms replacing pews. Dismas Houses also employ ex-convicts, especially if they hold degrees in social science, social services, or social work.

Dismas is the patron saint of criminals. As the story goes, while on the cross, Dismas repented his sins, and asked Jesus for redemption. He was not known for doing good deeds, and was crucified by the Romans for the commission of crime, and was never officially canonized by the church. Nevertheless, Dismas is the only human to be canonized personally by Christ. Meanwhile, St. Leonard is the patron saint of prisoners. Some convicts even wear medals around their necks commemorating these two saints.

Many local nonprofit secular companies also operate halfway houses in their communities. These are usually organized by entrepreneurial social workers. They purchase large old homes, run-down motels, or small apartment complexes and convert them into halfway houses. They tend to operate their facilities in a more informal, almost home-style fashion.

The advantage of halfway houses run by nonprofit groups is that there aren't any DOC correctional officers controlling your every move. But there are rules, and the organization must abide by the provisions in their DOC contract or risk losing a steady stream of clients. These rules are pretty basic. For example, residents are not allowed to bring alcohol or drugs into the house, or have sex on the premises. There are also rules about housekeeping, curfews, and being respectful to your fellow housemates. They may also require that you pay for room and board, especially if you have a job.

Operationally, nonprofit secular facilities are the most unstable of the bunch because they depend exclusively on the whims of the state or federal prison system funding. For example, the DOC or FBOP shuts them down for not requiring drug tests of inmates, or when a prisoner stays out all night and commits a crime, or if there are too many complaints from angry neighbors. Generally, people do not like a halfway house being located next door. This is generally referred to as the "Not in My Backyard" phenomenon.

## Halfway Houses Owned and Operated by Ex-Convicts

Our favorite halfway houses are run by ex-convicts. These tend to be the most user-friendly places, with few rules and little official supervision. Instead, the inmates monitor each other. They are assisted by ex-convicts with college degrees who are hired to be peer counselors. As former prisoners, they understand the many challenges their clients face. These institutions are also more likely to be trusted by the inmates, who tend to need role models and mentors more than guards at this stage of their journey. Besides, ex-convict employees know all the games and hustles that inmates run, and have little patience for fools who jeopardize the program.

If residents can't handle the relative freedom at this style of halfway house without breaking the rules—for example, getting drunk or high once too often—they are asked to leave. If they are belligerent or threatening, won't work to pay their bills, or refuse to help clean house, they are sent packing.

If they are unable to abide by the rules of the ex-inmate-run halfway houses, then their PO might reassign them to a different facility with more rules.

One very innovate halfway house operated by ex-convicts is Hope House in Kentucky. This company purchased a number of mini mansions on a street. Hope House took in alcoholics, drug addicts, and prisoners that had been denied or refused DOC or FBOP halfway house assignment. Inside prison the convicts had heard about this facility. When they got out of the joint they went straight to the house to ask for assistance. Every night they held Alcoholics Anonymous meetings in the backyard of the main building that drew a large crowd.

Most big cities have halfway houses representing the entire range of facilities described in this chapter.

## Halfway Houses for Women

Although some large facilities accept both male and female inmates, most women ex-convicts are assigned to designated female facilities. These are usually large homes in residential neighborhoods. They might even do double duty as shelters for battered women. Typically, the first floor is a common space, with the living room reserved for visitors during the day, another room for television or computers, a kitchen, and maybe a laundry room in the basement. Upstairs, depending on the size of each space, the women sleep two or more to a bedroom. The entire halfway house might accommodate 10 to 20 women.

In some smaller, more informally organized halfway houses, the women may be encouraged to live family-style in the house. Residents might plan meals, do the grocery shopping, and make meals together. The women take turns washing dishes, mopping floors, and cleaning bathrooms. Many small residential halfway houses for men function much the same way.

# Thinking About Halfway House Options
# While Still in Prison

Typically, when a convict "gets short," meaning he has less than a year on his sentence, he makes an appointment with his prison case manager to discuss his release plans. The case manager may offer a halfway house and decide the number of days the inmate will stay there. The inmate can either accept or reject the offer, although he is usually given little say in the length of time, location, or type of halfway house. He might request a specific facility, but there are no guarantees, as bed assignment is primarily determined by vacancy.

Even though there aren't any guarantees, it never hurts to put in a request for a particular halfway house. And while you're at it, it might be in your best interest to consider moving to a different city or state from where you came. A change of scenery is often good, plus it puts you at a distance from old temptations that may pull you back into a criminal lifestyle. Naturally, you will need to clear this with your PO, and you will have to balance this against employment opportunities and your family connections. If you have no commitments to a spouse or children, then it may make sense to move to a different city and state from where you were convicted of a crime.

Many veteran convicts who have been in and out of prison don't trust halfway houses. They know that some of these facilities have a high failure rate, unrealistic expectations for residents, and charge exorbitant fees for room and board. Some penitentiary convicts will actually refuse assignment to halfway houses, as they do not trust the correctional authorities to give them an even break, or they know they will screw up, violate their parole, and be returned to prison.

While you're behind bars, ask around. Many prisoners recently recycled back to the joint have up-to-date information about different halfway houses. They can tell you about rules, fees, and the way staff treat inmates.

## Arriving at the Halfway House

If you are assigned to a halfway house, you usually have 12 to 48 hours to report to the facility after your release from prison. It goes without saying: no stops at the bar or visits with your homeboys. The halfway house personnel might test your urine or subject you to a breathalyzer as soon as you walk in the door. *If you fail to arrive on time, you risk being returned to prison immediately.*

Once you arrive at the facility, introduce yourself to the staff, present your get-out-of-prison paperwork, and wait for directions.

Assuming you arrive during the day, you might be invited to meet with the correctional supervisor, facility director, halfway house manager, social worker, or case manager.

**Be courteous during this first meeting.** You can assume the halfway house knows you were coming and has received your correctional file, including commitment papers, pre-sentence investigation, and prison records. The correctional file may include complete copies or brief summaries of the same. However, do not expect the halfway house staff has read or even peeked at the file before your arrival.

**Do not ask about your mail, visits from friends or family, or your commissary account.** It may take a couple weeks to arrange for these things. You also will not be able to purchase, own, or drive an automobile while at the halfway house. So don't ask. You will probably not be allowed visits for a while. They may not even let you out of the house to look for work until you complete their orientation procedure. Remember: this isn't a vacation, and you're still in custody of the criminal justice system.

**Our best advice is this: be patient.** It may take a staff member some time to read relevant sections of your file before you can be assigned a bed. Staff may also be busy with other business, for example attending to the needs of various residents. While you wait, and depending on the type of facility, the personnel may ask you to sit in the hall, in a TV room, or on the front porch. At least waiting is something you had a lot of practice with in the penitentiary.

Eventually, you will be assigned a room, issued sheets and towels, and introduced to your new roommates. The residents will give you the lowdown on the place. Some of them will share their opinions, tell you what to expect, and warn you about particular rules and dangerous residents and staff. Listen, observe, and then make up your own mind about how to proceed. Try to stay positive. No matter how many rules they have and how unfriendly it may seem at first, most halfway houses are a big improvement over prison.

## Your First Visits with Family at the Halfway House

While in jail or prison, all visits were strictly controlled and observed by correctional officers. The prisoners had "no contact" or "limited contact" visits. At the halfway house, residents are allowed "full contact" visits. They are able to meet with family and friends in a room without direct monitoring by corrections staff. They can sit beside one another, hold hands, and kiss, as long as they don't get carried away.

Just like in prison, most halfway houses require all visitors to be on the staff-approved list. They may limit this to immediate family and legal counsel. The visitation rules are more relaxed at non-government-run halfway houses. Typically they let you go out as you please to visit family or friends, and there is no need to have visiting lists, hours, or procedures.

Most government-operated facilities have set visitor hours during which residents can receive guests. Visitors are not allowed to wander around the place on their own or to enter resident bedrooms. When you do receive a visit, keep it short and simple. You don't have much privacy, so you don't want the authorities or other residents to learn too much about your family and friends. Now that you are in the city, your family is much closer, so they can see you more often if they like. Besides, in a few weeks you may be able to go home for an evening or an entire weekend.

## Stepping Your Way to More Freedom

Most halfway houses use some version of a step system, where you earn more privileges and time outside the facility. The name of the steps might change or vary from one facility to another, but they generally follow this sequence:

1.  Arrival at the halfway house. Make sure you are on time, sober, and drug-free.

2.  Orientation, which may last several weeks. The halfway house may need time to receive and read your files. There may be residents that have such serious criminal records or reports of bad behavior while in the joint that they will not be released for work or school.

3.  Released to look for work or attend school. Once you find employment and demonstrate that you can keep your job or are attending classes at a college or university, you may qualify for evenings out with your family. Eventually, you may be allowed to spend a night at home with your family.

4.  Weekends at home. As a final step, you may get permission to stay a weekend at home with your family. Usually, the government-run halfway house programs will not let you spend the weekend at home with your girlfriend or boyfriend. They will probably require that you be married.

In general, how fast you progress through these steps depends on many factors, including your criminal convictions, the reports in your correctional file, your progress in finding and keeping a job, your payment of court-ordered and halfway house expected fees, how well you get along with staff, and the length of time you have left at the facility.

Unfortunately, you just have to get used to the idea that your criminal conviction, and the type and seriousness of the crime you committed, may be used against you. If the sentence is for contract murder, child molesting, or cop-killing, then you may progress slower through the steps. If you have a reputation as being a gang member or having been violent in prison, the halfway house may not want you on the street. If the police or district attorney raises questions about your return to the community, the halfway house may not be allowed to let you out of the facility at all.

In general, if you have a job and are making a good-faith effort to pay your bills, including court-ordered fines, restitution, child support, and bills for room and board at the house, then you will progress through the step system just fine.

## Finding Employment

Remember the job you listed in your official parole plan? Well, both you and your prison case manager knew that it was just made up, something to fill in the space on some bureaucratic form. The problem is, your case manager at the halfway house is sure to ask you about it. Just tell the truth, and move on. The staff know that most prisoners come to the halfway house with fictional parole plans.

It's important to keep in mind that prisoners tend to have a different attitude toward work than the average citizen. When people on the outside work, it's usually to support a family, to save for an important goal, or if they are lucky they might even have a career or profession that they love. Work release prisoners usually don't have any of these reasons for getting up in the morning and going off to a job that's usually eight hours of drudgery.

In addition, halfway house residents only get a fraction of their earnings. When an ex-convict finds a job—perhaps at a fast-food restaurant or doing telemarketing—her paycheck is typically mailed or electronically deposited to the work release center. What little money the inmates make is controlled by correctional staff. Much of their pay is deducted for room and board as well as court-ordered fines and restitution. A little may be set aside for the prisoner's daily expenses, and the rest is put in savings to be used when they are released.

More than likely, the halfway house will have some arrangements with local fast-food restaurants, car washes, telemarketing businesses, janitorial services, construction companies, and/or low-wage factories where they place residents in jobs. The halfway house may have a list of employers that consider interviewing ex-convicts. Many halfway houses also post job listings on a bulletin board. We talk more about finding a job as an ex-convict in Chapter 7.

The most important thing is to get a job (or stay in school), keep it, and try to save some money. You need to "get with their program" as best as you can. If you do this, there should be little reason why you will not be released soon. This is just another whistle-stop on your way home.

# Chapter 5

## Give Me Shelter

While at the halfway house, Joe explores possible living arrangements for when his six months are up at the DOC-run facility. He has to find a place to live that is acceptable to his parole officer (PO). Joe knows the PO will not likely approve of the invitation he has received from his sister and her husband to crash on their sofa—his sister is an exotic dancer and her husband is a biker with a criminal record.

Joe next considers staying at his parents' house, but he knows that would be a mistake, as he would have no privacy on the living room couch, and he would wear out his welcome in a week. Besides, his father, like his uncle and older brother, own firearms. So there is no chance he can stay with his immediate family.

Joe goes down the list of old pals and former girlfriends. It has been too long, he has lost touch, and, besides, most of them are married or divorced with children and have their own problems. And who wants an unemployed ex-convict straight from the joint sleeping in the guest room?

Joe will have to somehow save enough money at the halfway house so he has first month's rent and security deposit for a cheap apartment. The problem is he has no job and already owes the halfway house money for room and board.

## Living Arrangements

The most important thing you need when you get out of prison is a place to live. If you weren't assigned to a halfway house (which is another set of headaches; see Chapter 4), you'll need to find suitable living arrangements on your own. This will give you a little more time to find a more permanent place to live.

Let's assume you walk out the prison gate with no halfway house and go straight to the street. You'll need a bed that night, but you might not have any money to pay for a motel room. You need to call somebody—for example, your mother or brother—for a couch to sleep on. But this will probably only be a temporary solution. You definitely don't want to move in with your fast-lane buddies who party all night and sell drugs on the side. You need a stable situation where you will not be tempted to return to the wild side.

You cannot live just anywhere, especially not where people keep firearms. This includes your old man's deer rifle or cousin's shotgun. If your PO makes a "home visit" and sees a civil war musket hanging over the fireplace mantel, you may be busted and catch a new federal case (see Chapter 10).

If you do live with any friends or relatives who own guns or other firearms, they'll have to remove them from their residence and store the weapons somewhere else. And if you are pulling in an income, no matter how meager it is, show some initiative and buy a bag of groceries from time to time. If you have no money, then at the very least clean up after yourself and offer to mow the lawn or do some home repairs to help compensate your hosts. Offer to look after their children while they have a night out on the town. At the very least, try to be a good houseguest.

### Searching for Your Own Apartment

We recommend that you find a small apartment or rental house in a quiet neighborhood with a low crime rate and few police. Try to avoid the ghetto, barrio, tenderloin district, or trailer park. The problem is that you may not be able to afford anything better.

Your best bet is to look for a modest apartment or even a room in a middle-class community. Cover your tattoos, watch your language, keep your noise down, try to blend in with the locals, don't draw attention to yourself, and under no circumstances invite your old crook friends over. If you are looking for a place to live and are asked to fill out a rental application, you may get a rude surprise. Many landlords use applications that include the dreaded felony question. Just tell the truth.

Whatever you do, don't mail the application in or leave it with the receptionist. Go to the landlord's office in person. Ask to speak to the rental agent or landlord. Introduce yourself and shake her hand. Look her in the eye and use this as an opportunity to explain your criminal record face-to-face. At least this way the rental agent will see that you are well-dressed, have good social skills, and appear to be a reasonable person. If necessary, she can ask you additional questions about your employment and family situation.

## Surviving Criminal Background Checks

Many landlords will check out prospective tenants using online criminal background databases. They will also verify your employment and check history. They can run the checks without even telling you, so you might not even know why you are denied a rental.

One way around this is to have a good friend or relative whom you trust rent the apartment or flat in his or her name. For example, you might ask your girlfriend, brother, or sister to meet with the landlord and put the rental in his or her name.

Whatever housing arrangements you make, make sure it meets the approval of your PO. After spending many years in a prison cell and after being denied five other rentals, nearly any apartment will look good to you. You might make the mistake of renting a flat in a duplex where your downstairs neighbors are known crack dealers.

But your PO knows better. He may force you to vacate the premises. Not only will you have to move and lose your security deposit, but you also may be sued in small-claims court by the landlord for breaking the lease.

### Places to Avoid

Be especially cautious when considering large apartment complexes filled with unemployed people. Similarly, try to avoid housing where there is a lot of action in public spaces like in front of the buildings, or in the lobbies, hallways, or parking lots. Pay special attention to police activity in the area.

Some privately owned apartment buildings can be even worse than the projects. They may include a lot of "Section 8" tenants. These low-income tenants bring their vouchers to the rental offices and pay below-market rates.

Some laws restrict ex-convicts from living in public housing. You may even be prohibited from moving in with relatives living in the projects. If you want to live in one of these units, you need to research the law.

## Shelters and Soup Kitchens

If you cannot afford a place of your own, numerous organizations provide food and temporary lodging for ex-convicts who have been recently released from jail or prison. Some of these facilities are run by cities and counties. Others are administered by religious, not-for-profit, or for-profit entities (see Appendix B). It goes without saying that there is considerable variation in the way each one is managed and the quality of the living conditions.

## Utilities and Other Expenses

After you find a place to rent, you will need to arrange for utilities, such as electricity, water, and a phone line. Utility companies might perform criminal background and credit checks, but instead of denying you service for being an ex-convict, they might ask you for a large deposit.

If you go home to the same city you were originally arrested in and it just so happens that you stiffed the utility before you did your stretch, you may have to pay your outstanding bills before the company will turn the gas or electricity on.

You may have similar issues with the telephone company. We suggest you consider only having a cell phone, as it may be cheaper and more convenient than a land line. However, check with your PO about this: you may be required to have a land line, especially if you wear an electronic monitoring device.

## Bouncing Back and Forth

Joe and Jill may find that they are bouncing back and forth, sleeping in different places over the course of the first few weeks or months they are out of the joint. The fact of the matter is that when you get out of prison without money or job, it will be difficult to find steady employment and a stable, affordable place to live. You may very well be forced into temporary jobs and accommodations.

Be patient. It will take a while to settle into a regular job, a place to call home, and a new life. The important thing is to not give up or engage in any risky behavior. Be prepared for it to take you a while to figure things out.

## Worst-Case Scenarios

A large percentage of the prison population in the United States is made up of long-term inmates, the elderly, developmentally disabled, mentally ill, and sex offenders. These people have unique challenges when they get out of prison.

Long-term inmates—folks who were locked up for 20 or 30 years—often no longer know anybody on the outside, have no friends or family to help, and don't have anywhere to go. They end up homeless, eating out of a dumpster, and generally unable to seize the meager opportunities presented to them.

Many elderly prisoners are disabled, confined to a wheelchair or bed, and have no way to support themselves. They have absolutely no place to go. Eventually, they will end up sleeping in the street, in the city parks, in subway cars or stations, or eventually in a shelter.

The developmentally disabled or mentally ill may suffer a similar fate. In some cases, they may simply be transferred from prisons to mental hospitals or public health institutions. And if you are a convicted sex offender, you might find it very difficult to find any type of reasonable housing.

# Chapter 6

## Dealing With Your Parole Officer

Traditionally, prisoners rarely served every day of their sentence in prison. From the 1950s until the 1980s, most states and the federal government had some type of indeterminate sentence. How long a person actually stayed in prison was decided by a parole board. For example, a prisoner sentenced to 10 years might get out of prison after serving only one third or one half of their sentence. If the parole board let a prisoner out after five years in prison, he or she would do the remaining five years on parole in the community.

Since the 1980s, many states and the federal government have replaced indeterminate sentencing with determinate sentencing, which is sometimes referred to as "truth in sentencing." In most prison systems, this means there is no parole release; instead, a prisoner must serve 85 percent of his or her sentence.

Both Joe and Jill were sentenced to 10 years in prison and 10 years of community supervision. Prisoners call this 10 years "in" and 10 years "out." Under truth in sentencing, they are required to do $8\frac{1}{2}$ years in prison, and $1\frac{1}{2}$ years on parole. Then they begin serving their community supervision, a second sentence that follows the first.

## Joe and Jill's Second Sentence

Joe is released from prison after serving 85 percent inside on his first 10-year sentence. He will serve the remaining 15 percent on parole. He will then do 10 more years outside on his second sentence.

Jill has the same two sentences. However, she served 100 percent of her first sentence inside prison. Jill lost her 15 percent good time for disciplinary infractions. She left prison under mandatory release, which is also called *expiration of sentence*. Jill still has 10 years to do on the outside.

Both Joe's and Jill's second sentences will be supervised by parole authorities.

Typically, 50 percent of parolees will be returned to the can within one year, and 70 percent within three years. Most of these parole failures will be for technical violations of parole rules: failing to report to a parole officer (PO), testing positive for illegal drugs in their urine, not paying court costs or restitution, or being suspected of engaging in illegal activities. Only a small number of parolees will actually be returned to prison on a new conviction.

Generally, the longer a person is behind bars, and the fewer family members and friends who remain in touch with him, the more likely a prisoner will fail parole. The fact that many prisoners must complete many years of community supervision after their stint in the joint also contributes to high rates of parole failure.

This chapter gives you the tools you need to avoid parole failure and getting sucked back into the prison system.

## Starting Parole

When you get out of prison, and as you are completing your halfway house sentence, the DOC (or more specifically the Division of Probation and Parole) will require that a PO contact you. Usually they show up at the correctional facility during the final week of your stay to introduce themselves. You don't get to pick the PO. You are typically stuck with whoever shows up.

Many POs find themselves in the difficult position of having to perform the duties of a social worker while also serving as law enforcement officers. This means that their focus is on public safety, surveillance, and ensuring that their clients comply with the numerous court-mandated orders.

Increasingly, the POs' duties as law enforcement officers are being stressed over their social worker role. This trend may have something to do with the fact that in the past community corrections workers earned degrees in the fields of social work, psychology, and sociology, whereas today they are disproportionately drawn from individuals with degrees in criminology and criminal justice.

This means that, compared to in the past, probation and POs are more likely to cite probationers or parolees who do not comply with the court-sanctioned requirements. They are less likely to turn a blind eye or lend a helping hand.

After years in prison, it is hard to trust anybody, especially an officer. You might need to take a deep breath, listen carefully, and remind yourself not to judge a person by his official title or job.

## Getting a Read on Your Parole Officer

POs come in all different sizes and shapes and with different personalities. They might be great, good, so-so, incompetent, or "straight from hell." It's important to get an early read on your PO's personality and demeanor. This will make a big difference in how you treat him and the kind of treatment you can expect in return.

### Great Parole Officer

There are a lot of great POs. These are often the social worker types who become officers because they really want to help people. This does not make them naïve or stupid, however.

Hopefully, during your time in the joint you have come to realize that sometimes those who work in corrections really are nice, care about others, and want you to succeed. They believe that people can succeed in life if given a fair chance or a second chance. Maybe they talk and behave like the parent you never had. They might even give you appropriate advice on where to live or help you get a job.

## Good Parole Officer

The good PO is not great, but better than a so-so one. They may have a huge caseload and not much time to help you, but at least they bear no ill will toward you. They are relatively competent, have done their job for years, have seen just about everything, and "go by the book." To their credit, their heart is in the right place. If needed they might even bend the rules a little, cut you some slack, and maybe even a break, if you need it. But be careful about pushing them too far, or expecting too much, as this is outside their job description. After all, they are a law enforcement officer, and will not risk their jobs to save you.

## So-So Parole Officer

Some POs are police wannabes. They applied for police jobs, but for various reasons were not hired, so they took the next-best thing in their eyes and became POs. Some of them dream about moving from the state parole system to the federal system. At least with the feds they will make more money.

A lot of these individuals are decent folks, but they see the world in terms of good people and bad people. If you are saddled with this kind of PO, you need to be extra careful. Do not let them stereotype you as a bad parolee. You need to show them that you are serious about finding and holding a job or returning to school, paying your bills, taking care of your obligations, and staying out of trouble.

## Incompetent Parole Officer

Every parole office has one or more men or women who are straight-up incompetent. They might go through the motions, pretend to do their job, but they really don't care. Somehow they manage to graduate from college, but they just aren't that bright.

They may learn what little they know about crime and punishment primarily from watching television or movies. Like a lot of people, despite the time they spend at work, they are just not that interested in the problems that ex-convicts might have. When it gets down to it, they just do not want to associate or spend much time with their clientele. When quitting time comes around, they are the first in the office to leave.

You will be able to identify an incompetent PO when you meet him. He will smile, shake your hand, and then give you the same lecture he gives everybody about "just follow the rules and we will get along." He will be the PO who can't remember your name, locate your file, or respond to your calls or questions in a timely fashion.

His desk is a mess and there are stains on his paperwork. He does not know how to dress for the job, and he jumps every time the phone rings for fear that he will be asked to do something he either does not know how to do or does not want to do. He is also a little lazy.

To be fair, he might be a nice guy who just does not like his job. Maybe he would be happier teaching high school (probably nothing more taxing than gym), or working as a security guard at a retirement home. You can't blame him. Not many people like spending 40 hours a week meeting with criminals and ex-convicts.

Although he is incompetent, this can work in your favor, as he won't go out of his way to bust you for small infractions. Just show him the respect he so desperately wants. When you must meet with him, just give him the yes sir, no sir, thank you sir routine, which is the same demeanor that worked so well on prison guards.

Maybe he will even forget to pressure you to pay your restitution, or pay for another piss test.

### The Parole Officer from Hell

Unfortunately, you might get stuck with the "Parole Officer from Hell." This is a man or woman with an ugly disposition—an authoritarian who enjoys abusing and bullying parolees.

More than likely he is one of those police wannabes who wants to wear a uniform with a badge and carry a gun. He is totally frustrated because he keeps failing those police/law enforcement exams. Maybe he can't pass the physical or psychological examination. In the meantime, he hangs out with the local police at the "cop bar" trading war stories about the criminals he meets and complaining about the parole boards that so easily let ex-convicts out of prison.

His office, or more likely the cubicle he occupies, is different from the others. You will notice lots of photographs of him on the wall with the director, and internal awards he has garnered over the years. He hangs his bulletproof vest and helmet on the wall, ready and waiting for him to wear when he leads the "crash" team on a search-and-destroy mission to search a home and arrest a parolee.

Too bad for you, this guy has never understood that his job is primarily to help parolees make it in the community. Instead, he thinks he should "trail them, nail them, and jail them." This is the person who is "out to get you." Just don't take it personally; he is out to get everybody.

## Parole Officers Work Different Caseloads

The chief PO hands out work assignments. Usually he or she sorts clients into groups and assigns them to different officers. For example, a young inexperienced PO might receive a lot of easy cases, such as people on probation, first-time offenders, housewives, and corporate executives. These are the type of people who have steady employment and maybe even own their home. They are not likely to be hustling dope, using hard drugs, or gangbanging.

Another PO might get the standard caseload, which is a mixed bag made up of an assortment of people, young, old, male, female, light-weight, and heavyweight. These are parolees who could go either way, meaning they might be no problem or they may disproportion-ately be the ones who the PO cites with a violation next week.

Typically, the so-called hard-core cases are grouped together to be supervised by one of the more senior POs. These are the drug addicts, alcoholics, gang members, and folks with a bad temper. These ex-convicts are the ones POs have to watch closely, includ-ing visiting their homes and places of work and interviewing their neighbors and friends. Doing so can eat up a lot of time in the POs' busy schedule, but it's a necessary evil because these are the people who might hurt not only themselves but somebody else.

POs may also have special caseloads. For example, the chief PO or her immediate subordinate may assign one officer to the juveniles on probation, another to adults on probation, a third to women on probation or parole, with a separate person handling sex of-fenders or those convicted of DUIs.

Probably the worst job in the office is supervising sex offenders. These kinds of assignments can have subtle short- and long-term psychological effects on the parole agent. A PO who spends all day with child molesters and rapists can develop some unusual psycho-logical tendencies.

It pays to know what type of caseload your officer has. Over time you may determine this from what your PO talks about or what his other clients look like.

If you have a female PO under 30 years old, and her clients all dress like they have real jobs, chances are you have been grouped with the lightweights. If your PO strip-searches all clients, and meets with you with a second agent in the room or standing nearby, then your file has been mixed in with an intensive supervi-sion caseload.

## Parole Officers Often Feel Threatened

Keep in mind that POs don't have the easiest jobs in the world. Their clients are often hostile—and sometimes even violent— to them. Most jurisdictions allow probation and POs to carry weapons. Likewise, some community corrections workers (e.g., Maryland) are now wearing body armor when they make arrests or go into what they believe are dangerous situations.

## Staying Clean

While you are on parole, you are still considered to be in the custody of the DOC. Parole is simply an alternative way to serve a prison sentence. POs have the right to—and frequently do— search your residence. They can show up at your place of work or residence and ask all sorts of embarrassing questions, including asking your employer and family questions about your behavior, associates, and whereabouts.

POs are a suspicious lot, and they tend to think (often rightly) that parolees are up to no good and will go back into "business" (selling dope, burglarizing homes, stealing cars, etc.). A few parolees have no intention of giving up the fast life.

Some ex-convicts want to get back everything they lost while in the joint. They get some minimum-wage job to serve as a front, and then return to their former criminal activities. They return to what they know and attempt to reestablish their place in the illegal marketplace.

Although your friends and associates may have escaped the drag-net back when you first took a fall, since then they probably have come under the watchful eyes of the authorities. The bottom line is that you need to go straight, because you now have a criminal record. The cops have your photo, fingerprints, address, previous criminal history, and maybe even your DNA.

You're a "made man," made in the worst way. You're now one of
the "usual suspects," easily tracked or placed under surveillance.
You are subject to having your parole violated if you're even *suspected* of having committed a crime.

It is time you just made up your mind to give up the rackets
slinging dope or whatever hustle you know. You need to adjust
to a more modest, even boring, lifestyle, where you get up in the
morning, go to work, stay out of the bars, go to bed early, and
live within your means. And when all is said and done, try to have
some fun!

## The Life Cycle of a Parolee

All parolees change over time. A heavyweight criminal typically
matures out of crime, and gets old or simply too tired after years
in prison. He is too exhausted to plan another heist. He has finally
made up his mind to go straight, even if he has to live in a public
housing project, watch soap operas all day, and work a minimum-
wage job. The man has decided he is too old to do more time in
prison.

On the other hand, many young adults with relatively light criminal records—maybe car theft or bad checks—are just beginning
the sad journey down a road of criminal mischief. They have been
in jail, spent a year or two in some minimum-security camp, and
are now ready for a big-time penitentiary. These are the young
men and women who are out to make a rep for themselves. They
may even want to see their picture in the paper. Unfortunately, this
is just what will probably happen to them.

The fact is, there is no way to really predict individual human
behavior. The young gangbanger sitting next to you in the parole
office waiting room might one day wise up, accept some advice,
and go to college. The fair-haired mother of two serving probation
for shoplifting may go home tonight and murder her husband in
his sleep. There is just no way to tell.

## What Kind of Advice Can We Give Those on Parole?

When you meet with your PO, it's a good idea to put some effort into your appearance, but avoid looking too flashy. If your body is covered in jail-house tattoos, wear a long-sleeve shirt.

Remember to brush your teeth that day, get a haircut, and take a shower or bath. Be exceptionally polite. Say good morning or good afternoon. Show the PO that you can carry on a casual conversation. Casual chatter is one of the superficial ways that a parole office gets to know you.

And no matter what you do the rest of the time, *do not drink or use illegal drugs the day you report to the parole office!*

Be sure to promptly pay your fees for reporting, urine tests, court costs, child support, and restitution. Even if you do not agree with the amount that you were ordered to pay each month, or if you have some questions whether past payments were properly credited, now is not the time or place to make a scene or to bring your attorney. Just make the minimum payment.

Don't play games with the PO. Keep him informed with respect to where you work and where and with whom you live.

If you think you are going to get laid off or be fired, tell your PO. If you can't pay your rent and expect to get evicted next week, let him know. If you're having marital problems and think your wife might walk out on you or call the cops, discuss it with the PO. POs do not like surprises. You are far more likely to be treated sympathetically by your PO if you keep him informed.

You will need official permission to move from one residence to another, change your job, get married or divorced, or change the town, city, county, or state you live in.

You can ask to transfer your parole supervision to a different jurisdiction, but it can be a long process. Generally, you need a good reason, and the new parole authority has to agree to accept your case. Moving from one part of the state to another is usually easier than asking to have your case transferred to an entirely different state; however, the Federal Interstate Compact Agreement does provide parole departments a means to request that a case be transferred to another state.

## Travel Restrictions

While serving time on probation or parole, your travel may be restricted to one county, a number of adjoining counties, or the state. Federal parolees may not be allowed to travel outside of the federal court district where they are supervised. You may need written permission in the form of a letter from your parole office to travel outside the jurisdiction.

When you travel, you must have this letter on your person. In part, this is for your own protection. For example, if you drive to Disney World with your family and get pulled over by a state trooper, you may need to show the cops the letter to avoid getting arrested. When they run your plates or check your driver's license on their squad car computer, they may determine that you are on parole in another state. Without the letter, they may decide you have "jumped parole" and are on the run.

The parole office may also stipulate additional travel restrictions for certain clients. For example, sex offenders might not be allowed to visit parks, schools, daycare centers, or any place where children may be present. Former drug dealers or prostitutes may be prohibited from frequenting certain high-crime streets. Literally, a PO will say, "If I catch you walking or standing on such-and-such street, you will go back to prison." Most parole agents will not allow you to go to a bar. Some warn heavy gamblers they will be violated if they are seen in a casino or purchasing a lottery ticket.

The bottom line is this: read the rules of your parole very carefully. If you have questions, ask your parole agent *before* taking that trip to Montana. Otherwise, your next trip might be back to the slammer.

# Chapter 7

## Finding Work

Given the high unemployment rate and the economic woes facing our nation, finding a good job can be difficult for anybody. So when you factor in a felony conviction and a stretch in prison, getting a decent job can seem impossible.

If you're staying in a halfway house or other community correctional institution, the first place to start looking for a job is at the facility itself. They usually have a list of employers that hire ex-convicts and other desperate adults who no one else will employ. Don't expect anything fancy: these are the typical fast-food restaurants that hire kitchen and cleaning staff, telemarketing firms hiring phone staff, roofing contractors, landscape firms, and temporary services operations. Almost all of these jobs pay minimum wage and have no benefits. Some are just part-time or seasonal. Ex-convicts right out of prison typically work minimum-wage, dead-end jobs.

This chapter deals with some of the challenges involved in finding an appropriate job and, once you land one, holding on to it. You'll learn how to deal with the tricky questions about criminal history that appear on most job applications. We also discuss interviews and how to work your way into a better-paying job.

## Bus Tickets and Lunch Money

Recognizing the difficult financial situation community prisoners find themselves in, some halfway houses will advance small amounts of cash to some inmates. The convict must ask for the money and specify that it is going to be used to pay for transportation and meals. To make sure you pay it back, the halfway house usually deducts what you owe from your first paycheck. Some facilities will not hand out cash, but they will give residents bus tickets, bus passes, or subway tokens.

## Finding Suitable Employment

Most prisoners will lie to the parole board about a lead they have on a job they'll get with a friend or relative once they get out. Everyone knows this is all part of the game inmates must play in order to get parole.

Even if you do have a job lined up, you might find once you get out of prison that it really isn't suitable—perhaps because it's on the other side of town and you don't have appropriate transportation to get to it, or because it's in another city that you're unwilling or unable to relocate to.

Sadly, many ex-convicts honestly think they have a job lined up, only to find that it has fallen through when they get out of the joint. Often it's simply the case that their friends or family members are either unable or unwilling to follow through on their promises when the time comes. Or perhaps your brother-in-law or friend of a friend had a job opening last week and may have another one in the future, but not just today when you need one.

No matter how hard it is, you gotta get a job. So now that you know the obstacles you face, you should take steps to overcome them by following the advice in this chapter.

### A Little Help from the Feds

A felony conviction will seriously impair your ability to find almost any kind of reasonable work. Recognizing that employers tend to shy away from hiring convicted felons, the federal government gives incentives to businesses that hire ex-convicts. The Work

Opportunity Tax Credit (WOTC) program gives tax credits to employers who employ "qualified veterans, ex-convicts, high-risk youth, vocational rehab referrals, qualified summer youth employees, qualified recipients of some federal aid programs, or an 18- to 24-year-old resident of a federally designated empowerment zone or enterprise community."

## Take a Long, Hard Look in the Mirror

Do you need a haircut and new clothes? Do you look like the kind of person someone would hire? If you don't, then you need to put some effort into your appearance before you start pounding the pavement in search of a job.

It is absolutely essential that you "dress for success" when you apply for jobs. If you are applying for blue-collar jobs, you will need a clean, wrinkle-free, well-fitting shirt, pants, and work boots. If you hope to interview for clerical work or a retail position, you will need a suit and dress shoes, or at least a nice pair of khakis and a collared shirt.

So where do you get the clothes? Don't count on wearing the old clothes your spouse or mother has stored all these years. They probably won't fit anymore, and even if they do, they are likely to be out of style, worn out, moth-eaten, or just old-looking from just hanging in the closet for so long. Suits and coats, like people, tend to lose their shape over time.

If you are close with your family, ask them if they will buy you a few things and drop them off at the halfway house. Be sure to give them the proper sizes—for pants, shirts, and shoes. Better yet, ask them to loan you money so you can go shopping on your own. That way you can make sure you get something you feel comfortable in and that fits you properly. After all, your sizes probably have changed since the last time you bought new clothes.

Assuming the halfway house will let you out the door for non-school- or work-related purposes, you might also visit the Salvation Army, Goodwill, St. Vincent de Paul, or similar second-hand stores to ask for clothes. Many of these charitable organizations are more than happy to help men and women just home from prison.

Ask someone at the cash register if you can speak to a manager. Be honest with her about your situation—that you have just got out of prison and need clothes to start looking for a job. More than likely, she will tell you to go ahead and pick out all that you need. Usually the items will be free, but you might be asked to work a few hours in the store loading or unloading donations.

By the way, these charities might work the same deal when you need furniture, bedding, appliances, a television, and kitchenware to furnish your own apartment. Usually they want you to work a couple days or a week or two, depending upon how much stuff you take.

Whatever you decide to do, if you're living in a halfway house, make sure you know the rules regarding personal property. If possible, get and save receipts for anything you purchase or are given. You don't want the correctional staff to become suspicious about the origins of your new clothes and household goods. And besides, you probably won't have a lot of room to store many possessions.

Here's one final piece of advice regarding your appearance: although you want to celebrate your freedom by getting a new tattoo or some sort of visible body piercing, try to show some restraint. Many businesses will not hire employees with visible tattoos or stainless steel or titanium embedded in their flesh. And don't forget that law enforcement can use piercing and tattoos to identify you.

## Finding Job Openings

Most people start looking for jobs by picking up the local newspaper and reading the classified ads. If the ad seems promising, you might want to call the place to get more information and find out if they are still accepting applications. Then you may need to travel to the business and fill out a job application.

Online employment databases, however, are now the most prominent excellent source for job listings. If you do not know how to use a computer or have no access to one, go to the local library and ask for help. Popular job websites include www.monster.com and www.careerbuilder.com. You can also look up jobs listed on state unemployment office websites.

Often you can fill out an application online. Some halfway houses have computers set up to be used exclusively for job searches, complete with relevant "bookmarks" of favorite websites and instructions. They may even have a staff member or inmate who helps residents with this task.

Keep in mind that some residents—for example, people convicted of sex, white-collar, computer, or corporate crimes—may be expressly prohibited from using computers. If you are unfamiliar with computer job searches or you do not have authorization to use a computer this way, you might ask family or friends to do the Internet job search for you, print out what they find, and bring it to you at the halfway house.

Many jobs are filled through word of mouth. An employer asks an employee if she can recommend someone for a job opening. The employee has a friend or relative who needs a job and puts him in touch. Obviously, having been behind bars you are at a disadvantage when it comes to word-of-mouth job hunting. But it's not too late to start "networking" with family and acquaintances who might be willing to help you get hired where they work. All you have to do is tell everyone you know that you are looking for work. One of your contacts may have information about a business that is hiring and will recommend you for the job.

## Filling Out a Job Application

If your highest degree is a high school diploma or a GED and you are applying for a blue-collar—so-called unskilled or semi-skilled—job, you will more than likely need to fill out a job application. Every employer has a different form, but the format and questions are usually pretty much the same.

If you are filling out a paper application, make sure you complete the entire form neatly using black or blue ink. You might be able to take the blank applications to the library or halfway house to type in the answers, although handwritten applications are usually acceptable for blue-color jobs.

Be sure to use your official name on the application—no abbreviated versions, nicknames, or aliases. If you are hired, your employer will need your official name for payroll, taxes, and Social Security. Also, you will need to give your address, which may be the halfway house, and a phone number where they can call you or leave a message.

Be prepared to answer the questions regarding past work and education experiences. You may wish to write these particulars down on a separate piece of paper to carry along with you from place to place as you apply for jobs.

If you have prison vocational or education courses or certificates, mention them here, especially if they are relevant to the job. For example, if you are applying for a job in a restaurant, and you worked a couple of years in the prison cafeteria, put it down.

Some employers know that prisoners may have acquired work skills in the penitentiary. They may have hired ex-convicts in the past who learned their skills in prison. Former inmates may be able to cook, bake, landscape, do carpentry, lay bricks, do masonry work, or perform basic clerical duties. Prospective employers are especially impressed by men or women who acquired skilled occupations working in prison industries.

When you get to the question that asks, "Have you ever been arrested for or convicted of a felony?" write: yes. For many reasons, you have no choice. First, you should never lie about anything on a job application. We know other people lie; for example, they embellish or exaggerate their work history. They will probably even get away with it. As an ex-convict you will not get away with lying, because the employer will already be suspicious and ready to question your honesty. We suggest you not make anything up.

Second, when you come to the part about your previous work history, you're not going to be able to explain those wide years-at-a-time gaps in your employment record. In addition, both your halfway house and parole officer (PO) will call your employer to ask about your job performance, so your boss is going to find out anyway. Finally, many, if not most, employers, both in the private and public sector, do criminal record searches, and they do not need your permission.

After completing the application, politely ask to speak with the boss, manager, foreman, or head of human services or personnel. If you simply leave the application with the secretary or on the front counter, more than likely you will never get a call back. If you are told the boss is busy or unavailable, ask if you can wait. If you are told no, ask for an appointment.

Whatever happens, never leave the completed application with a subordinate. Hang on to it and return, with application in hand, on the day and at the time when you can expect to meet face-to-face with the person who interviews and hires.

When you meet the manager, introduce yourself. Then say something like, "It is a pleasure to meet you. I hope you have a few minutes to look over my application for employment." Then look him in the eye, extend a handshake, and give him your application. Wait patiently while he looks it over.

Remember, the supervisor is a busy person, so do not be surprised if she is interrupted by numerous phone calls, customers, or other employees. Wait until she reads the very top of the application. Hopefully, she will see your name and then ask you into her office for an interview.

If she stands there reading the entire application, ask her for an interview before she makes up some excuse to send you away. You may have to ask her for an interview before she reads the felony question.

## Submitting a Resumé

If you have a college degree or are applying for a white-collar or professional position, you will probably be required to submit a resumé. In general, resumés are for professional, technical, or managerial positions where people are paid salaries, which is a set amount per week, month, or year. In comparison, most blue-collar workers are paid by the hour, or possibly by the piece on a factory assembly line, or with wages and tips in service jobs.

Numerous books and online sources have been written on how to write a resumé. Resumé writing help is also available through social service agencies and job centers. Take advantage of these if you can.

The big advantage to a resumé, especially for someone just out of prison, is that you generate the content, so you don't have to include any mention of your criminal record. This means you can submit your resumé and receive an interview without the employer knowing you are a felon or just got out of prison. Of course, any close reading of your resumé may invite some questions about the gaps in your employment history.

It may be easier to get an interview if you have a resumé. In fact, we suggest you prepare one and make many copies to give to all possible employers. This way you have a carefully composed and typed document containing all your important information when you visit businesses to complete their standard application. Some organizations may even accept your resumé in lieu of their application, but don't count on this. They may have corporate reasons why all prospective hires must complete the same application. At the very least, you can use the information listed on your resumé to fill in the details on the application.

All resumés should include your present contact information at the very top. Follow this with a paragraph about education, then a few paragraphs about previous employment, and then finally a few sentences about jobs skills and qualifications. One page is a standard length for most resumés. Use high-quality ink and a font of at least 12 point, and print on a laser printer. Business center stores like Fed Ex Kinko's have resumé kits with selections of high-quality paper stock and envelopes. Remember to type out envelopes if possible, attach appropriate postage, and mail from a post office so they arrive faster.

Many employers now encourage applicants to submit their resumés as e-mail attachments. We even know employers who have, on occasion, hired some individuals with a good resumé after only exchanging e-mails and phone conversations.

## Using Letters of Recommendation

Sometimes it's helpful to have a couple of letters of recommendation from appropriate individuals attesting to your trustworthiness and/or commitment to the job. These should not be from your close relatives such as your wife, father, or sister. Sometimes a member of the clergy, rabbi, or former employer may be useful as letter writers, providing they know you and your circumstances relatively well.

Sometimes these individuals can mail the letter of recommendation to the prospective employer on your behalf, or they can create a generic letter that you can leave along with your application. Any letter of recommendation must present you in a good light and be as specific as possible. Letters of recommendation that are too general are not that helpful and can actually work against you. Be sure to have a good supply of them available when you make your rounds.

## Handling a Job Interview

Assuming that you dressed appropriately, that you look reasonably fit and ready for work, and that your application is neat and complete, you may get an interview. In large part, whether you actually land the job depends on how you conduct yourself during the interview. Most of what we tell you is just plain common sense. Always stand or sit with your shoulders and back straight and your head held high. Smile, and show some confidence. Try to use the same language, body language, and cultural cues as the person interviewing you. Pay attention to the words you use, avoiding convict slang and swearing. Never speak prison or street talk during the interview or, if you get the job, at work.

As with any job, you need to sell yourself and convince the employer to give you a chance, not because you need work, but because you can do the job. A good employee is not a liar. If you are asked to explain your criminal record, time in prison, long absences from the workforce, or any other tricky questions, just keep it brief and tell the truth. Hopefully, if you've done what we advise, and the person has an open mind, you'll receive some attention. Whatever happens, thank the person for her time and consideration. You never know—if you are polite, honest, and sincere, she might call you later and offer you the job.

The bottom line is, whether you submit employment applications, resumés, or both, you will have to inform the employer that you are a convicted felon before you accept the job or position. There is usually no way around this while you are still in "constructive custody" of the criminal justice system, which means serving a sentence, be it in prison or in the community. If you hide your prison record and get hired, the employer will eventually find out from your PO or the halfway house, and then you will probably be fired on the spot.

Remember, there are two types of lies: those of commission and those of omission—the former is telling an outright lie and the latter is concealing facts that people have a reasonable right to know. Besides the fact that you want to start out your new life of freedom being a straight and honest person, lying on a job application is often legal grounds for immediate termination. We have heard of individuals who, after years of devoted service to a company, are fired when the new boss digs up the individual's original application in personnel and discovers an error or so-called "white lie."

Also, keep track of the places where you filled out and submitted applications or mailed resumés, if only for the simple fact that the halfway house, PO, or judge may want verification you are actively searching for employment. One way to do this is to photocopy each completed application that you submit. This will help you build a file to demonstrate to your PO that you are complying with your parole condition by pursuing a job. This may require you to leave the site and photocopy the application. So be it. You may also wish to gather the business cards of the people you speak to. You need to accumulate appropriate documentation to protect yourself.

## Electronic Jackets as Stumbling Blocks to Seeking Employment

Community prisoners are often tracked by computer information systems and returned to prison when they fail to comply with court orders to pay restitution, fines, or child support; don't take their prescribed medication; or don't do the community service they are sentenced to perform. Surveillance protocols now include reporting by employers, teachers, and medical personnel. If the probationer or parolee does not show up for work, school, or medical treatment, he or she is often returned to jail or prison.

The community correctional penal machinery, once intended to support and assist cons' re-entry into society, is now used to supervise and monitor a growing number of men and women released from prison. The U.S. Department of Justice, law enforcement, and the courts keep criminal history records on every con and ex-convict, and they sell this information to the public. These are used to do background checks for employers, landlords, loan officers, and even utility companies.

Both public- and private-sector employers run criminal background checks, usually without your knowledge. They do not need your permission to do so. All they need is your name and date of birth. They may pay a company to do the search, or do an online search of court records themselves.

A considerable amount of what most people automatically assume to be private information is available to law enforcement agencies and private businesses throughout the United States. These records, including pre-sentence investigations (PSI), court records, even prison inmate central files, can be found online for free, or purchased through government offices for a modest fee.

So don't be surprised if your prospective employer decides to do a criminal background check. If he does, you can be sure he will be asking you questions about your incarceration.

## Jobs Related to Your Crime

It only makes sense that most employers will not hire you if your crime is related to their line of work. For example, if someone went to prison because of theft or robbery, the hiring company doesn't want them handling money. Likewise, if your crime is a sex offense, they will not hire you to work in a day-care center or school. If your offense is for bank fraud or embezzlement, forget about working in a financial institution. If you had a drug conviction, pharmacies, doctor's offices, and hospitals are off limits. And some companies don't let *anyone* who went to prison work the cash register or interact with customers.

Why? It's not because they dislike you or maybe don't trust you; it is typically because their insurance/bonding company will not allow it.

Despite the background checks and employee practices, don't give up! We know lots of convicted felons who have eventually overcome these obstacles. If you work hard and show an interest in advancing in your job, you may find an employer that champions your cause. Once people get to know you well, they may go to bat for you and open doors for you into the occupation you desire.

## Keeping a Job

When someone decides to offer you a job, be sure to thank her sincerely. She did not have to take a chance on you. Report to work on time every day, and do your job the best you can. You need to go to bed early, get a decent night's sleep, and get a good breakfast before work. Do not walk into work hung over from drinking, or yawning from too few hours of sleep. At the very least, don't tell your boss or co-workers the real reason why you look disheveled or are tired. No matter how modest the wages paid, do what the boss says. And if you want to keep your job, do it with a smile and positive attitude. More than likely, your employer can replace you easily, so don't give her any reasons to.

You need this job more than the company needs you, at least until you complete your time at the halfway house. The general rule is to work every job for at least one year. Never quit a job until you already have another one lined up. Then, you thank your boss, and always give your employer at least two weeks' notice.

Most bosses will give you a good work reference if you did a good job for them, give them appropriate notice you are leaving, and wish them well on your last day. Given that your work history is ancient history and that you have a prison record, these references are more important for you than they are for most people.

At work, don't run your mouth off, especially about jail, prison, police, or parole. Nobody will understand what you have been through, and most don't want to know. Your co-workers have their own problems and couldn't care less about yours.

Be friendly, but avoid being buddies with your co-workers. For the most part, keep to yourself and just focus on doing your job as best you can. Do your work and go home. Do not socialize with your co-workers after work. Do not go to the bar after work to drink beer and shoot pool. Just tell your co-workers you need your sleep and have work to do at home.

Do not tell any of your colleagues at work anything you wouldn't want your PO to know. They may be casually or officially questioned by your PO at any time. If they lie to a law enforcement officer, they can be arrested for "obstruction of justice." Provided you never told them you are on parole, or you did but they don't know the rules of parole or they care about you, they may well tell the PO about the good times you enjoy together after work.

The halfway house staff or PO does not need to see you drinking, catch you with booze, or have you fail a breathalyzer test to bust you. If one person at work tells him you have been to the bar, even if you were drinking soda pop, you are likely to be sent back to prison.

If you socialize with employees afterhours, eventually they're going to know that you just got out of a correctional institution, and the next thing you know you may get fired. Be careful about sharing your convict history. Once the word about you gets out, one or more co-workers may turn on you. There are a lot of self-righteous folk who think they are better than ex-convicts. Besides, if anything is stolen or goes missing at work, or if the work gets messed up, you know who they will blame.

## Getting Paid

In general, most community corrections facilities do not want residents to carry extra cash, as they are concerned that the parolee might tempted to spend it on drugs or alcohol. Usually, depending upon the rules at a given facility, you will be instructed to ask your employer to mail your paycheck to the halfway house.

Some facilities go so far as to require employers to write out the check to the halfway house agency or company. This is so the halfway house can cash or deposit the check in an account. They may even use direct deposit, which means the employer mails or e-mails the paycheck into a checking or savings account at a local bank. The halfway house will control your money and probably make deductions for room and board charges, program fees, court-ordered restitution or fees, and child support.

Although you may not like these policies and practices, you can trust that the halfway house will not steal your hard-earned money. Hopefully you can negotiate the amount of deductions they take out of each check.

## Types of Employment

If you are on parole, you will need a W-2 form and steady paycheck to show your PO. A W-2 means you cannot be self-employed, operate your own business, peddle old junk on eBay, sell paintings at art fairs, or work for Amway, Fuller Brush, or Kirby Vacuum Cleaner doing door-to-door sales on straight sales commission. You need a W-2 form paycheck once every week, bi-monthly, or once a month that states your hours, gross pay, deductions for taxes, and net pay.

You probably do not want any door–to-door sales jobs, even if you are paid company wages or salary. Door-to-door is just too danger-ous for ex-convicts. If a crime is reported in the neighborhood—for example a break and enter, burglary, or home invasion—one of the first things police investigators do is interview door-to-door salespeople.

If a crime happens in the area you've been working, you become an instant "person of interest" or "usual suspect." Next thing you know you are hauled off to the city jail, charged with a crime you didn't do, and persuaded to fess up in return for no trial, just a parole violation and an express ride back to the joint.

In addition, the halfway house needs to know exactly where you are when you are working. For this reason, they usually won't let you deliver newspapers, distribute mailers, or drive a truck long distance "over the road." We know one "owner operator" who lost his truck to the bank when his PO would not allow him to drive out of town. He wanted to live in his semi-truck and catch up on delinquent payments by delivering cargo to freight terminals. He ended up taking a job in a warehouse unloading trucks while his own rig was repossessed. As things turned out, this was better than violating parole rules, being sent back to prison, and losing his marriage and children.

This is why they want you to work at McDonald's, Burger King, or even a carwash—any place of business with a permanently fixed address and phone. They don't care that these places have poor working conditions and terrible pay.

So even if you worked as a truck driver, carpenter, or electrician before you went to prison, don't be surprised if the halfway house forces you to take a minimum-wage job flipping hamburgers or working a telemarketing phone bank. You need to work for an established business with a telephone and address, and to report every day so that you can be observed working by the parole authorities. You may have to swallow your pride to remain free.

Try to avoid seasonal, part-time, or casual employment. In these situations, the boss usually calls you up in the morning and lets you know whether he will need you to work that day. If conditions outside are bad (rain or snow), you don't work. That's one good reason why most construction jobs, outside painting gigs, or roofing jobs are probably inappropriate.

In addition, the halfway house may not know where you are if you work construction. Of course, you might think you could overcome the halfway house's objections by simply keeping them up-to-date on the addresses of construction sites. It depends upon the facility. Some halfway houses may be smaller operations, have fewer restrictions, and be able to accommodate your needs. But many have a rule that no work release prisoners can work construction, because they simply don't want to deal with the complexity of verifying your daily work location. They simply have too many people to keep track of every day.

Your halfway house and PO want to see that both the hours you work and the wages you are paid are consistent. This means they want you working for an established business where records are kept of hours you worked and what you were paid. In most states, parole offices actually require that you submit to them a report each month declaring how much money you made and from what sources. They then compare your declared monthly income with your standard of living or lifestyle. If you appear to be living beyond your stated income, they will start digging a little deeper.

POs are like cops assigned to supervise you and your activities in the community. As their caseload may be 50 to 100 parolees, they see all kinds. For example, they have supervised gangsters, drug dealers, crooked lawyers, and criminal corporate executives who, upon getting out of prison, have plenty of money and don't want to work at Wendy's. Maybe the gangster wants to take sports bets on the phone, while the drug dealer sells pot to his friends, and the crooked lawyer and criminal corporate executive just want to sip martinis and play golf all day. They think they can use cash to pay their bills at the halfway house and parole office and avoid the humiliations and restrictions imposed by community supervision.

The fact is, the parole authorities use employers to help keep track of what you do, where you are, and how you make money. It may bother your PO if you are making more money than him, enjoying yourself, having a good time. Some days it feels as if the parole authorities want you working a minimum-wage job. This may even appear to be part of your punishment.

POs may not even like you working as a waiter or waitress in a lunch café or family restaurant where you receive tips for services rendered. The halfway house does not want you spending your tips on drugs or saving it up to escape to Brazil. Yes, parolees have been known to get out of prison, reside in a halfway house, and then work a straight job to save up enough money, only to make good their escape to a foreign country.

## Don't Be a Fall Guy or Gal

You also don't want to work at any establishment where people use or sell alcohol or illegal drugs, or where gambling takes place. Quite often, you won't know what's going on behind the scenes in these businesses until it's too late. When the heat comes down because of some illegal activity that is happening on the premises, your managers or co-workers may well hang it on you, the ex-convict.

Don't be a patsy or fall guy. We've heard stories of legitimate-sounding businesses that purposely hire ex-convicts only to have someone to put the finger on when the place gets busted. This could be a company marketing vacation deals, selling time-share contracts on beachfront condos, or boiler-room sales of stocks and securities. Although they pay only commission, the halfway house lets you take the job because the company has a regular address. These crooks hire you knowing they are only a step or two ahead of the feds, and will be folding the business in the next few weeks. One day you come to work, the boss is gone, and the FBI is waiting for you. The company moves on to another city and reopens under a new name. Meanwhile, the cops are sweating you in the county jail, thinking that with your criminal record, you have to know something about the operation.

Maybe the worst place to work is a used car lot or auto dealership. One ex-convict told us about getting a job at a used car lot where they turned back odometers and sold flood-damaged cars with new titles. Another parolee worked at a new car dealership that got busted for selling stolen auto parts.

A third ex-convict shared with us his tale of woe about being hired without a sales license to sell new cars. He didn't know the dealership was selling people new cars and then stealing the autos back a few days later. The ex-convict was arrested when an elderly customer returned to the dealership to buy a second family sedan with his insurance money. It was a big dealership, so he wasn't surprised they had the same color and equipment package.

A few weeks later, the gentleman was driving the car, looking around for his favorite lighter to light his cigar. He inadvertently reached between the front seat cushions and discovered a familiar book of matches. Looking closely at the matchbook cover he figured out he had purchased the same car twice. He called the cops. They checked the VIN numbers on the car and compared it with the phony title. The ex-convict car salesman spent the next six months in the local slammer, waiting for the FBI to break the case wide open and decide he was an innocent bystander.

## Turning Menial Jobs into Better Ones

Just getting out of the joint, you have to start somewhere. After being paid 25 cents an hour in prison, almost any minimum-wage job at $7.25 an hour looks good. So you take the job at the fast-food restaurant. They stick you in the back, away from the customers, because you are not allowed to work the cash register and handle cash. So you learn to run the french-fry machine, assemble different types of hamburgers, to prep, clean up, take out the trash, and clean restrooms.

You're an ex-convict. You know how hard it is to get a job, to find an employer who has the courage to take a chance on you. Your boss is a good guy, expects a lot, and treats all the employees— including you—with respect. The first few weeks on the job were rough, but then it got easier: you learned a routine. The weeks turned into months, and then years. This job saw you through the halfway house, then years on parole. Every six months you got a small raise. After five years on the job you were making $10 an hour, which adds up to $400 a week, or $20,000 a year.

Meanwhile, you watch the high school kids come and go. They work summer vacation, and then go back to school. Eventually, you are allowed to work the cash register, and then you are promoted to become team leader, in charge of training new employees. Older and a little wiser, you come to like your job. Then one day, your boss asks you to stay and help him close for the night.

Later he needs your help totaling up the day's receipts. He then gives you the money bags and asks you to drop them in the night deposit at the bank. The next morning he promotes you to manager.

The moral of our story is that employers know that ex-convicts, if given a chance, may become loyal employees because they have fewer options in the labor marketplace and may appreciate the opportunity to be trusted. After all, most people just need a routine, a job to go to every day where they are appreciated, a chance to learn new skills, make a little more money, and eventually an opportunity to climb a few steps up the corporate ladder. Even a small retail business can offer a person the chance to convert menial labor into something a little better.

## Enlisting in the Military?

Many ex-convicts automatically assume that their criminal conviction precludes them from enlisting in the military. But this isn't necessarily the case. The military keeps changing its enlistment standards. As long as we are fighting two or more wars at the same time, the armed forces might even be interested in you. If this really interests you, we suggest that you consider visiting a recruitment office to explore the possibilities. Typically, as long as you do not have more than one misdemeanor or felony charge, you can enlist.

# Chapter 8

## Going Back to School

Prison is an ideal place to begin preparing for college. Convicts have a lot of time to read and study, their room and board is provided, and for the committed student there may be few distractions. Prisoners who begin taking college courses in prison on their own initiative are essentially reinventing themselves and planning for a bright, new future.

Although ex-convicts often make great college students, they face numerous obstacles when applying to institutions of higher education, including gaining admission to the institution, receiving financial aid, being admitted to student housing, and deciding on majors and careers.

In this chapter we provide information to help you navigate the higher-education labyrinth. Our goal is to show you how you can go to college and get a degree, so you have a fighting chance of getting a good job in the workforce after you are released.

## Are You Ready for College?

Reading serious books while still in the joint is the most common way of preparing for higher education. If you are still in prison, start going to the library on a regular basis. We suggest you read major newspapers like *The New York Times* or *Washington Post*, college textbooks, nonfiction, and self-help books like this one. Most correctional facility libraries have inmate clerks who can help you find the books you need to read.

Perhaps you can complete one or two college-level courses in prison. Typically this is done through the mail. Very few correctional facilities allow inmates to take online classes, as they don't want inmates using the Internet. They are worried that cons will use the web to do business, surf for porn, or get information to construct weapons or explosives.

Reading college textbooks or taking correspondence courses often starts inmates thinking about going to college. And doing these things can give you a head start on completing a diploma or degree.

But don't worry if you haven't taken any college courses in the past. In terms of academic preparation, all you need to be ready for college is a GED or HSED. You probably won't even have to take a college admissions exam such as the ACT or SAT. Many universities waive those requirements for applicants over 21 years old.

If you can read at a twelfth-grade level, have reasonably good command of the English language, and have basic computer skills, like using a word processing program, the Internet, and e-mail, you are academically ready for college. Like a lot of students, you may still struggle with math and physical science courses. The fact that you are a bit older, and have seen a bit more of adult life, may actually give you an advantage in some social science and humanities courses.

You need to be realistic about what you can afford, even with financial aid. In general, the cost to attend public universities is usually less than half the price of most private schools. This is because public universities are supported in part with state revenue. Your best value, where you get the most for your money, is a public university in the state where you have resided for more than a year and therefore qualify for in-state tuition rates.

You have to figure out what will work for you in terms of your family obligations, social commitments, location, and what you are looking for in a school. You need to collect and read information about different campuses, consider your options carefully, and then make an educated choice.

## Choosing a College

One of the first decisions you need to make is whether to attend a technical school, a local community college, a small liberal arts college, or a large university. Most technical and community colleges are less expensive and offer a wide variety of part-time programs. Some tech schools offer high school courses, vocational programs, and certificate completion programs. Community colleges may offer the same plus the first two years of academic course leading to an Associate's degree. Most small liberal arts schools offer a four-year Bachelor's degree in a variety of majors.

Many college students attend regional state universities that offer a large number of Bachelor's and Master's degrees, and possibly Ph.D.s in selected subjects. Every state has at least one large university offering all three degrees in many subjects and enrolling thousands of students.

Some students prefer smaller campuses, which may be more user-friendly. For example, it takes less time to learn your way around a small campus, and to find your classrooms and a quiet place to study. Small schools may also be more convenient for commuters who drive to campus every day and need a place to park.

On the other hand, you may like a large campus better, if you want to blend in with the crowd and remain anonymous. Thinking ahead, as an ex-convict, you may like college, and want to plan on completing advanced graduate degrees. These will help you overcome the prejudice you will find in the job market. The bigger the school, the more likely they are to offer the graduate program you want.

Large universities have more prestige. As a graduate of a large, well-known university, you will find many alumni in the community, some of them employers. This may help you in your future career. Besides, it can be fun to live on or near a large college campus, where you might meet people from all over the world, learn from famous professors, and attend an occasional football game.

Be careful about unaccredited schools, colleges, and universities. Although it may be easy to enroll in these "institutions of higher learning," prospective employers might question their authenticity and rigor, especially if a couple of years down the road your new prospective employer asks for your official transcripts and the school has gone out of business. Likewise, religious-based schools may appear to be exceedingly welcoming and offer you a great education. You need to consider what kind of impression graduating from one of them might have on future bosses and co-workers.

You don't want to get a Mickey Mouse degree from some educational institution that nobody respects. It can actually prevent you from obtaining some jobs. Beware of highly advertised colleges that make it sound so easy to obtain a degree. You can't buy a college degree on the Internet. The value of a college degree is closely related to the academic reputation of the institution.

Our advice is to discuss your plans with family, friends, and acquaintances who have attended college. Collect all the relevant information you can from various schools. If you can either visit campuses in person or investigate them online, make sure to ask a lot of questions.

## Former Prisoners You Can Read

Prison has helped produce numerous famous authors. While you were behind bars, perhaps you were introduced to some well-known convict authors. These include Miguel de Cervantes, Fyodor Dostoevsky, Alexandre Dumas, Antonio Gramsci, Victor Hugo, Aleksandr I. Solzhenitsyn, and Leo Tolstoy, all celebrated European authors who had served some time in captivity. You may have read the published works of convicts who helped to challenge or change the social or political systems of respective countries, like Mahatma Gandhi, William Reich, George Jackson, Eldridge Cleaver, Malcolm X, Nelson Mandela, and, of course, Martin Luther King. We also suggest you read our edited book *Convict*

*Criminology* (2003), which includes nine chapters by ex-convicts who are now criminology or criminal justice professors.

We know the public tends to think convicts are all illiterate high school dropouts. The fact is you know better, as you have met many intelligent men or women in correctional facilities. Studies show that the intelligence level of the prison population tends to mirror the general population of the country. It's all a matter of how people choose to use their intellect.

## Completing a College Degree

Many so-called "traditional" students (ages 18 to 22), both in prison and the "free world," take years to finish college degrees at large state universities. Very few finish in four years, even those attending classes on a full-time basis and living on university campuses. A four-year degree is now really five or six, depending on finances and academic ability. Yes, some students still graduate in four years, especially those who attend private schools. Still, most working-class students, who have to work jobs to pay their own way, take five or more years to finish college.

"Nontraditional" (older) students now make up a growing population on many college campuses. These are older men and women pursuing higher education later in life, maybe after a career crisis, divorce, military service, or stretch in prison. Many university professors know these students to be above average—even gifted— individuals who are serious about their studies.

### Will You Be Welcome on Campus?

Regrettably, over the years, as tuition rates have climbed, many universities have come to resemble middle-class country clubs for young adult students and professors. You can walk around all day and only see white suburbanites, most of whom look like they just graduated from high school or just walked off the pages of a Gap or J Crew catalog.

Most of the students have grown up in suburbia or small towns, and have few street smarts or experience with courts, jail, or correctional facilities. Mostly this is because they are young and have just begun their adult lives. Given where they come from, they are not prepared to understand where you have been, at least not yet.

Nevertheless, you will make friends with students. If they are new on campus, like you, they may not know many people, and they may be looking to make new friends. Look for students sitting alone in the student union or library.

Even though you may be closer in age to your professors than to your fellow students, don't assume that your teachers will want to befriend you. Many professors have little patience or understanding of the hard journey you have traveled in life. Besides, even if they wanted to, professors are usually way too busy to give you a lot of personal attention.

At top-tier research universities, professors may not even want to talk with their undergraduate students, at least not outside the lecture hall. They prefer to spend their time in laboratories or research institutes, with the Ph.D. students they supervise and mentor. At smaller regional state universities, where professors usually do less research, some may make a considerable effort attending to the needs of their students. If you want a lot of personal attention, you probably want to go to a small liberal arts college or regional state university for your Bachelor's degree.

## Minorities on Campus

Many African American, Hispanic, Asian, and Native American students complain about the almost exclusive white middle-class atmosphere on many college campuses. Despite university mission statements and the pictures of people of color prominently displayed on university promotional materials and websites, you will probably find very few minority students on most college campuses. The exceptions to this are the working-class technical and vocational schools, so-called metro campuses in urban areas, and the Historically Black Colleges and Universities.

Unfortunately, while many universities talk about multicultural awareness and acceptance, they have been less than successful at recruiting, retaining, and graduating minority students (and faculty) in large numbers. Of course, part of the explanation is the rising cost of tuition, room, and board, and the dreadful high school graduation rates for African, Hispanic, and Native American students.

As a response, nearly all universities, and to a lesser extent smaller colleges, employ counselors who recruit and advise minority students, women, older adults, people with disabilities, and veterans. While each of these groups has separate concerns and needs, most campus communities try to make them feel welcome. Different campuses have been more or less successful at helping these students.

## Ex-Convicts Are an Invisible Minority

It should be no surprise that very few universities devote resources to recruiting ex-convicts. Hardly any campuses have recognized the growing population of former prisoners that now attend university, live on campus, and study in lecture halls. This is reminiscent of the way Jews and women were treated on college campuses during the 1920s, and African Americans were perceived on college campuses in the 1950s, where lecture halls were filled with almost exclusively white men.

At that time, many state university systems maintained a separate campus for blacks and women. The university's unstated policy was to placate and segregate them.

Eventually, through the passage of civil rights legislation, universities were forced to end their segregation policies. Slowly, black students and women were allowed to attend all state universities, play on athletic teams, and be admitted into medical and law schools. The battle is by no means over, but as a society we've made a lot of progress.

We think of ex-convicts as an "invisible minority." They come in many colors. Their status as ex-convicts is not immediately obvious. In part, this is the fault of ex-convicts who hide, cover their tattoos, and conceal their criminal record. Understandably, most want to put their past behind them and be treated just like any other student. They also are very aware of the blatant stigma associated with being an ex-convict.

The problem is that universities need to know about your ex-convict identity in order to give you appropriate academic advising. You deserve their attention and assistance just like any other student who pays tuition. We suggest you be honest about your past with your academic advisors.

## Anticipating Common Problems

As an ex-convict, you will suffer some of the same prejudices and biases that other minorities have had to struggle with for years on college campuses. You may run into many obstacles with admissions, financial aid, and housing. Some university staff will be intimidated by ex-convicts. One door after another will be slammed in your face. At least if you know that door is going to be closed in your face, you might catch it in your hand before it breaks your nose. Who knows, you might even kick it in with your boot.

## Admissions

When it comes to applications, every school is different. Some require you to apply online, while others will accept handwritten paperwork.

Regardless, most colleges require prospective students to pay an application fee of $20 to $50 and submit it along with their applications. However, many colleges will waive this fee for financially needy students. When you apply to college, ask for a financial waiver on the admission form.

In general, you will find the admissions office has a lot of useful information designed for new students. Visit the office and pick up some information. Be sure to verify your admission status before you start your first semester. Usually you receive a letter in the mail.

## Financial Aid

Most people coming out of prison who have been admitted to a college or university qualify for a full package of student financial aid. This is because the amount of financial aid you receive is determined in large part by the previous year's income, as declared on a federal income tax return. Because you were in prison and probably had no income, and were not required to submit a tax return, you should qualify for the maximum financial aid possible. This can include scholarships, fellowships, grants, and loans. More than likely it will be a combination of grants and loans, and possibly federal work-study. You should receive a letter from the financial office notifying you of what has been awarded.

Making sense of your financial aid package can be one of the biggest headaches you'll have to deal with as you make your preparations for entering college. To help you make sense of it all, here are some definitions:

- **Grants** have no repayment obligations.

- **Loans** must be paid back, and can carry different terms, including interest and repayment schedules. Most are zero interest while you are in school and then relatively low interest after graduation. The loans are usually repaid over a 10-year period, but you can ask to have the repayment period extended.

- **Work-study** is a federal program in which you are paid minimum wage or a bit higher to work part-time on campus, such as in the library, residence hall, or cafeteria.

- **FAFSA** stands for Free Application for Federal Student Aid. This is the federal application that all students must complete if they want to be considered for student aid. You can go online and download the applications. Pay close attention to the deadlines for submitting your application.

At the beginning of your first semester, you usually pick up your financial aid check at the financial aid office, or the money is deposited directly into your bank account. The university deducts money for tuition, fees, and maybe housing and meals if you are living in a campus dormitory. This leaves you with money to buy books and pay for other living expenses. If you need additional money, you might find a part-time job on campus, or in a nearby business.

We give three important warnings about financial aid:

First, the funds are meant to pay for your expenses at school, not for a car, new clothes, court-ordered restitution, or to catch up on your child support. While legally you can use the money for whatever you want, you need to carefully budget to pay your expenses while in school. You must register for and complete a set amount of credits per semester to stay eligible for financial aid.

Second, university study is hard work. You will need to attend classes, study every week, write research papers, and take exams. At many universities, a large number of students fail classes and are thrown out of the university because their grades are too low.

Third, even if you need additional money to pay your bills, you will probably not be able to handle more than a part-time job. If you withdraw from the university without completing the required credits, or flunk out, you will probably be required to repay your existing student loans before you get more.

Finally, there is federal legislation that denies financial aid for people with drug convictions. (If you were convicted of homicide, rape, or bank robbery, you are not affected. Go figure.) However, the law is subject to interpretation and has been revised several times. The FAFSA application says you must "not have a drug conviction for an offense that occurred while you were receiving federal student aid (grants, loans, and/or work-study). This means that most felons, even drug offenders, are eligible for federal student aid when they get out of jail or prison. As the law may change from year to year, we suggest you consult the FAFSA website (www.fafsa.ed.gov).

We strongly encourage you to tell the truth when you complete your FAFSA. Then, research the current law on the Internet or ask the university student aid office for more information.

### University Housing

Don't be surprised if you are denied access to student housing. Even if the university will let you register for classes, they might not give you a dormitory room. That's because some campuses run criminal background checks on some or all students applying for housing.

We know one male graduate student who was asked to move out of the dormitory when the university found out about the particulars of his criminal record. We know of a female prison inmate who was approved for admission and financial aid, but when the university staff at the student housing office found out she was coming to the college from prison, they denied her housing.

## Deciding on a Major

In general, you need 120 credits or more for a Bachelor's degree. Each class is worth approximately three credit hours. Universities usually suggest that you complete 60 general studies credits before you decide on a major.

We encourage you to meet with an academic advisor as soon as you arrive on campus. Be honest with the advisor about your felony status so that she can appropriately advise you in your selection of a major. Many professional fields are closed to ex-convicts. If you are a convicted felon, you should not major in education, social work, nursing, medicine, or law, because you will probably never be allowed to get a license or enter the professions; a criminal record stands as a formidable barrier. Sure, you might be able to get a degree in one of these fields, but you won't be able to work in those fields after you graduate.

## Education

Education is probably the worst academic major for an ex-convict to choose. Elementary, middle, and high schools don't hire convicted felons to work as janitors, let alone teach children. We don't want you to waste two years or more of your life, completing credits toward a degree in a K12 education program, just to be denied employment.

The only exception to this warning is if you get a degree in education and teach English as a Second Language outside of the United States. (That is if you can get a visa to enter and work in another country with your criminal record.) If teaching is your passion, then we suggest you consider working at a technical or community college and/or university. As an ex-convict, you cannot teach children, but you can teach adults.

Of course, if you want to teach above the high school level (for example, at a tech or community college) you will need at least a Master's degree. If you want to teach full-time at a university you will need a Ph.D. In general, the rule is that you need to have completed at least one degree higher than the students you teach.

## Social Work

If you decide on social work, which would mean pursuing a BSW or MSW, just know that you may have a difficult time getting a state license to practice in your profession. However, without a license you still may qualify for many social service positions, including working with juvenile and adult ex-offenders.

We have heard countless stories about ex-convicts who have been discouraged from majoring in social work by social work advisors. They may tell the ex-convicts that they do not have any more spaces available in the program. Or they might explain that they don't think it is a wise investment of their scarce resources, because the student will never be licensed. In reality, their advice is probably based more on fear of ex-convicts and a general desire to keep former prisoners from entering the program.

## Nursing, Medicine, Dentistry, and Pharmacy

While you could finish a degree to become an LPN, RN, MD, DDS, or RPh, the medical-health professions do not welcome ex-convicts. For one thing, drug addiction is a very big problem for medical-health practitioners, and they worry that you will succumb to this kind of temptation. For example, they don't want you to get a job in a pharmacy administering drugs. They think you might steal the inventory and/or get addicted. If meds go missing, then all employees are under suspicion.

Another issue is with liability and insurance coverage. Insurance companies do not want to take risks with insuring medical clinics, hospitals, or pharmacies that hire ex-offenders. While it is possible that a medical establishment may pay extra money to bond a particular job candidate, don't count on it. You will have a difficult time getting a job in a medical clinic, hospital, or pharmacy. You'll even have a hard time getting a job as a physical therapist, x-ray technician, lab tech, kitchen helper, or maintenance person in a health clinic.

## Business Degrees (e.g., Accounting, Finance)

As an ex-convict, it is difficult to get any job that involves working with money. You already know that if you get hired by a fast-food restaurant or retail store, your boss does not want you anywhere near the cash register.

Many university schools, colleges, or departments of business, which can be very popular with undergraduate students, won't even let you major in the subject if they know you are an ex-convict. If you do decide to pursue a Bachelor's or Master's in business, accounting, or marketing, just be forewarned that most corporations run criminal background checks, and eventually you will have to explain your past. If you get a degree from an Ivy League or elite university (e.g., Harvard, Yale, Princeton), you might get interviews and maybe even be hired at a small company.

Of course, getting an education in business could help you with your entrepreneurial plans such as opening your own retail or service company. If you have capital, connections, and a good idea for an innovative product or service, you could be successful in business on your own. Just be careful you do not capitalize your new business with illegal money. You don't want to catch a federal racketeering (RICO) case.

## Law

Given your experience with the criminal justice system, law might seem to be a natural choice for a new profession. Certainly many ex-convicts have studied criminal law. They have used this knowledge to fight their case or have a better idea of the context of their detention.

Law schools, like medical schools, have felony questions embedded in their application materials. No matter how high your undergraduate Grade Point Average is and your score on your LSAT exam (used to screen law school applicants), you will have a very difficult time being admitted to a decent law school.

You may have more luck with the least prestigious schools. The lowest-ranked private law schools may not care whether you have a criminal conviction for admission. They may just want your tuition money.

Let's say you manage to complete a law degree, and pass the Bar exam; you still may not be accepted to the Bar (the licensing authority in each state). Unfortunately, a criminal conviction serves as a formidable barrier to becoming a practicing lawyer. Many ex-convicts with law degrees are not admitted to the Bar, and so can't practice before a court. They end up working as paralegals doing legal research for law firms or corporations and making much lower salaries than lawyers.

## Criminology/Criminal Justice

In many respects, one of the most appropriate fields of study for ex-convicts is criminology/criminal justice. Keep in mind, however, that studying this subject may make for a very uncomfortable experience, at least initially. In class you will be sitting beside other students who want to be cops and who may be hostile to ex-convicts. They want a job arresting and "putting away" all the bad guys. Additionally, your chances of getting a job with law enforcement, prisons, or probation or parole departments are next to zero.

On the other hand, many criminal justice students graduate from college and have careers in social service agencies working with juveniles, mentally ill or challenged people, or prisoners in the community. We know of many social service agencies that hire ex-offenders with college degrees.

Finally, maybe you are interested in doing research in criminalogy and/or justice or teaching the subject at the community college or university level. Unlike many of your fellow students, instructors, and professors at the university, you have firsthand knowledge of the reality experienced in courts, jails, and the prison system. You may want to consider completing an advanced degree in criminology or criminal justice.

## Challenging the Academic Bureaucracy

We want to remind you that as a taxpaying citizen you have a right to attend public colleges and universities, just like everybody else. Provided you meet the academic requirements and can pay the tuition, you should be admitted. Nevertheless, being an ex-convict complicates everything.

You will encounter bureaucratic barriers erected by universities, colleges, schools, and departments that attempt to prevent you from completing your studies. We encourage you to keep your head up, be patient, pay your tuition, and get good grades. All the hard work *will* pay off.

## Inviting Convicts to College

We introduce a new model for a free college prison course designed to serve prisoners anticipating release from prison within two years. The course serves as a bridge for prisoners to exit prison and enter college. The model çan be easily started by undergraduate or graduate criminal justice programs at universities within a relatively short distance from state or federal jails or prisons.

The courses prepare prisoner-students to make an informed decision about enrolling in a college or university upon their release from prison. The incarcerated students learn the academic skills they will need to succeed in college.

The model includes a number of innovative ideas. First, the classes are free for prisoners and are taught by undergraduate or graduate students, who earn credit for their work. Deploying pairs of students in this fashion means universities do not incur the expense of reassigning faculty to teach the classes.

In addition, the program does not require criminal justice professors as sponsors. Faculty from many academic disciplines (such as anthropology, business, English, and psychology) may implement the program with relatively little or no support from the university administration. Courses in African American history, anthropology, Latino studies, women's studies, and social work might be especially welcome.

University administrators talk a lot about affirmative action and diversity. Meanwhile, many college campuses are nearly exclusively white, while prison populations are disproportionately black and brown. Universities that are seriously concerned about attracting minority students should look to their nearby prison. In the prisons, they will find many minority men and women waiting for an invitation to remake their lives with the help of higher education.

Prisons and universities have many traits in common. Most are state-funded, and the institutional populations are in many ways the same—mostly young men and women in need of training and education. One way we can all serve the community is for universities and prisons to work together to reduce recidivism and help prisoners to become productive citizens. Besides, we all know it costs the state less to support one college student than to return a man or woman to prison.

Prisoners make good college students. In the joint, they have a lot of time to catch up on their reading. They are already institutionalized, accustomed to living in dormitories, and know they have a lot to learn if they want to avoid returning to prison.

# Chapter 9

## Family, Love, and Sex

For better or worse, we are all the products of our environments. Hopefully, you were raised by a family that loved you. Unfortunately, not everyone grew up with parents or guardians who knew how to serve as good role models, properly monitor their children's activities, and give them the appropriate guidance and direction they so desperately needed.

Today in America nearly half the children are born to mothers without husbands. The presence of both a mother and father does not guarantee a happy, healthy, and well-adjusted child. However, single-parent families (whether fatherless or motherless) tend to have the lowest incomes in America. Neighborhoods with the highest rate of single parents tend to be poor, with lots of street crime, and high numbers of people cycling through correctional facilities.

The destruction of the traditional American family is both part of the cause, and in part the result, of the dramatic increase in prison populations. The rate of incarceration for African Americans, Hispanic Americans, Native Americans, poor whites, and unemployed Americans is so high that communities in some urban areas have been depopulated of adult men. As the jail and prison population increased, so did the number of children without fathers. Some of these kids grow up on the streets and join gangs in search of respect and unmet emotional needs traditionally provided for by a family or male role models.

In this chapter we discuss the options available to you with respect to reconnecting with your wife, husband, or ex, ways you might be able to create or rebuild your family, find love, and, if all else fails, at least have a little sex.

## Prison Separates Families

Wars on crime and drugs tear families apart. The bad guys and gals, if they don't die in a drive-by shooting or get shot by the police, more than likely will be sent to jail or prison. Either way, with so many young adults in correctional institutions, families slowly fall apart. Men and women returning home from years in prison may have serious difficulty reconnecting with their families.

Millions of children growing up in the United States have at least one parent who is locked away in a correctional facility. These kids are raised by spouses, uncles or aunts, grandparents, or foster parents. They may visit their father or mother in jail or prison a few times a year.

Add to this the thousands of women who are pregnant when they go to prison. In some states, women give birth wearing handcuffs and leg irons. A day or two later, the newborn babies are either picked up by the immediate family, placed in foster homes, or put up for adoption. The children may not have an opportunity to even bond with their biological mothers. In other words, they never had the chance.

In correctional facilities, many convicts cry when they think about their children, and how they will not be home to see them grow up. Some prisoners wait anxiously for news from home. They tape photos of their spouses and kids on their cell walls. As the years pass they collect more photos. They write the names and birthdates on the back of the pictures so they won't forget.

Old convicts will tell the younger convicts they have to learn to give up what they left behind in the free world. In prison you can't control what happens outside. You can't protect your children or help your family. If you are to survive your time behind bars, you have to focus your attention on what goes on around you.

Nevertheless, some inmates hang on to these hopes and dreams when they know they should let go. Despite their mistakes that brought them to prison, they cling to the belief that one day they can still be mommy or daddy. Meanwhile, the children grow up.

## Family Visits in Prison

If the prisoner has a family, more than likely they will come to visit for the first few years. Convicts get haircuts and iron their uniforms, trying to look the best they can for their husbands or wives, boyfriends or girlfriends, and children. In the prison visiting room they change diapers, watch cartoons on television, and play board games with their kids. If the weather is nice, they might play outside on a swing set. Once a week, under these artificial conditions, as best they can, they act like a normal family and do their best to enjoy their time together.

Eventually, the wife or husband realizes that a 10- or 20-year sentence is for real. There will be no appeal, and no miracle from heaven. She has her own needs, be they economic, emotional, or physical. He has no way to help her pay the rent, or keep her warm at night. She eventually hires an attorney to prepare the paperwork for a divorce.

The convict saw it coming. Her visits became less frequent, and with each meeting her demeanor was a little less engaging. Three years into his bit (sentence), all illusions gone, she no longer comes to see him. He knew separation would mean that divorce was inevitable.

At mail call, the convict eventually receives the legal-size envelope and knows what it means before he summons the courage to look inside. His buddies persuade him to retreat to the relative safety of his cell before his anger causes him to hurt himself or somebody else.

## Learning About Parenting in Prison

Parenting is a skill handed down from one generation to the next. You have to understand what a good mother or father is before you can be one yourself. Many mothers and fathers in prison didn't know how to be good parents in the first place. They were too young and too poor. Hopefully, they can use their time in jail or prison to become better parents.

Locked up in correctional facilities, they might meet other inmates who, despite their personal misfortunes, were good parents. These moms and dads will talk about their kids and share stories about their families that will help others learn much-needed parenting skills. In addition, most prisons offer classes on parenting skills to help inmates succeed in their second chance at parenting after they are released.

## Civil Death

Prisoners in many ways are like ghosts. In correctional facilities, they feel like they are no longer part of the real world beyond the walls. By law, inmates suffer "civil death." They can be legally stripped of property and assets. In some states they have no right to contest divorce or child custody proceedings. While in prison they are not allowed to conduct business, sign contracts, or do business by mail or phone. For example, inmates cannot own, manage, or operate a business, apply for credit or loans, or transfer securities or financial resources. If they get caught operating a legal business while behind bars, they can be charged with a disciplinary infraction and locked in solitary confinement.

Most convicts with long prison sentences will lose their spouses and children. Their husband or wife will file for divorce and sole custody of the kids. The convict will have few if any avenues of dispute or redress. Their families give them up for dead. Convicts call this "burying the ghost." In effect, family members inherit homes, cars, and bank accounts, without having to pay for the funeral or cemetery plot. The man or women is buried alive in prison.

## Remarrying in the Joint

A few convicts will get married while still in the joint. To do so, a convict needs written permission of the warden. The bride and groom get married in the correctional facilities' chapel. The wedding reception is in the visiting room. Of course the groom does not wear a tuxedo, although the bride may wear a traditional wedding gown. Usually the wedding party is very small, with just a few people. After a brief ceremony, the official papers are signed, and the reception is limited to a few hours together in the prison visiting room. The wedding cake might be a few cupcakes from the vending machines.

In general, the convict population likes marriages. Not because they get to attend, but because they are pleased to hear that life goes on behind bars. They find some small measure of hope in the fact that, despite the years of separation, people are interested in marrying prisoners.

Even prison administrators and parole board members like weddings. They know that a good marriage can help domesticate even the wildest desperado. Sometimes, couples will marry inside prison hoping it will help the prisoner get a transfer to an institution closer to home, a parole date, or a reduction in sentence. Prison wardens are known to give a man a transfer to an institution closer to his new bride. The convict might think of this as a very thoughtful wedding present.

Just like on the outside, some prison marriages work, while others do not. Some women who marry male prisoners will tell you that while he is incarcerated at least they know where he is, and not with another woman. They come to the correctional facilities every week to visit their new husband or wife. Some wait many years to consummate the marriage. There are no honeymoons for inmates.

## Pretend or Pseudo Families and Gang Affiliations

Loners don't do well in prison. Human beings are social animals. That is why many convicts, especially women, replace their free-world family with another one in prison. Most prisoners make friends and alliances in correctional facilities, whether for protection, friendship, or family.

### Cliques and Gangs

In male high-security penitentiaries, inmates form family-like affiliations for mutual protection. Affiliation may be decided by race, ethnicity, criminal occupation, or simply who you cell with or make friends with the first few years inside. Convicts might seek affiliation based on their former criminal profession—mafia soldiers, bank robbers, or drug dealers—hanging together on the yard and eating at the same table in the mess hall. African Americans may have cliques (pronounced clicks), which denote their street number or "hood" (neighborhood). Mexican Americans may talk about the convicts they hang out with in prison as their "car," the same men they would ride with on the street.

Some prisoners hook up with a gang or criminal organization in prison, and then go to work with them when they return to the free world. Many organized criminal groups recruit new members in jails and prisons. All of the so-called super gangs—the Crips and Bloods, Hells Angels, Latin Kings, Aryan Brotherhood, and Black Gangster Disciples—are based in part on recruiting membership inside jail or prison. Gangs are family for many men and women who have spent long stretches in juvenile and adult prison warehouses.

### Losing Your Prison Family

People leaving prison after many years may experience a profound sense of loss. They miss the friends they made behind bars and camaraderie their "second family" provided.

Years later, a convict might run into an old prison buddy on the street. They might reminisce like two sailors who served together on a ship. The ex-convicts will shake hands and possibly hug and talk about their time in the joint. They might ask if other mutual acquaintances got out, or recall some event they still think about. Sometimes one ex-convict might even help another find a job or provide a lead on suitable accommodations.

## Reconnecting with Your Family

You understand it is inevitable that your family has changed while you were in prison. Making peace with these changes may help to lessen any pain you might experience. Still, you know going home will not be easy.

### Coping with the Destruction of Your Marriage

Some marriages are meant to last. Still, very few survive the incarceration of a wife or husband. You are very lucky if your husband, wife, girlfriend, or boyfriend stuck by you. Some are just good-time spouses, who move on when things get rough. They forget their marriage vows, particularly the saying "till death do us part." More than likely, if you were married when you went to prison, it was over long ago, probably in the first few years of your incarceration.

Did you hear through the grapevine that your wife or girlfriend is now living with your best friend? Maybe you learned that she dyed her hair blonde and is working out at the local gym. For better or worse, prison has a strange way of reshuffling the deck, of sorting out your life without you present.

Maybe your ex-spouse was just as wild as you years ago. She didn't want to work a boring straight job for wages. Still in her 20s, she enjoyed magical substances, counting large stacks of cash, driving a new BMW, wearing expensive clothes and jewelry, and vacationing in Hawaii and Europe. When the good times ended and you went to prison, she became the good mom who never used illegal drugs or lived in the fast lane. She used the remaining illegal proceeds to buy a house, send the children to private school, and buy more fancy clothes to catch a new husband.

You thought she loved you, and if you provided her with cash and savings to pay her bills while you were away, that she would welcome you home. The reality is your ex-spouse loved the good times more than you, and wanted more of the same without you. Maybe you underestimated her greed.

When you went to prison, she moved to another state, buried your memory with booze and men, and when she found somebody who could keep her in the style she was accustomed to, she divorced you. You can guess what your ex-wife is saying to your children about you.

Hopefully, by the time you do get out of prison you will have forgiven your spouse for whatever he or she did while you were in jail or prison. You might walk or drive by her house and see if there is a yellow ribbon tied to the front gate or a welcome-home sign in the window. But don't count on it. Remember, life marched on while you were locked in a cage.

## Going Home to See Your Ex

If she invites you into her home, be careful or the visit will be cut short. This is an emotional time, and it's difficult for both of you. At the very least, don't ask who helped her pay the rent/mortgage, covered the utilities, or stocked the refrigerator with groceries. Don't inquire about the strange shoes under the bed, coat in the closet, or car in the driveway. Try not to get crazy when your kids address another man as Dad, even in your presence.

You were absent without leave, missing in action, and nobody really knew when you might return, living or dead. So your wife divorced you, took a boyfriend, had a few affairs, or just screwed around. Unless you married an angel or a saint, anything is possible.

If you happen to be introduced to her new boyfriend or husband, do your best not to hit him. Avoid being violent, even if he initiates it. If you have to, turn around and walk out the door. These are the kinds of situations that can land you back in prison in a heartbeat.

While it may be too late to rescue your old marriage, it may still be possible to begin a new relationship with your children. You need to realize that the situation is out of your control. Your ex-wife and kids will decide if and when they want to see you. Hopefully, they will still love you, want you, and need you in their lives.

You might find another scenario more inviting: As you climb the stairs to the front porch of your ex-wife's house you smell the sweet odor of marijuana. The front door of the house is wide open. You knock on the screen door, and call, "Anybody home?" She must have seen you getting out of your car. You hear her voice, "Just a minute."

She meets you at the front door with a big fat joint in her hand. "Welcome home, honey." She appears genuinely happy to see you, and gives you a big hug. Even though it is 11 in the morning, she offers you a beer. As the memories slowly come rushing back, you remember how much fun you once had together. You recall that you once even loved one another. She looks great. You hope she is between boyfriends. Maybe she missed you.

You are welcomed home. Eventually, the conversation comes around to the big question. Where are you staying? She suggests you might spend the night. Her smile says this will not be a night on the sofa. You hope you are up for the activities.

The next morning, she tells you in no uncertain terms that your relationship will have to be very different. You will both have to forgive and forget a lot of life and love that happened while you were away. While you were in prison her life did not stand still. Don't ask her about the men, affairs, or boyfriends who came and went.

As a single mom, she survived on low wages, one step ahead of eviction notices and the bill collector. She did what adults do when they are lonely and need another person for emotional and financial support. It is not her fault you disappeared for a few years. Besides, she just shared her bed with you. She wanted you to know what could be. You have to decide if you can still love her as she is now.

Then again, sometimes lovers break up and learn how to go on as just friends. You realize your marriage is really over, and what she does is her own business. Your concern is this: will she allow you to see your children? Hopefully you can keep a job, pay child support, and find a way to be a friend to your ex-wife.

## Relationships with Your Children

When men and women get out of jail or prison, they typically search for their children. While you were locked up, your kids grew up without you. Considering the fact that you are a felon and ex-convict, and the stigma attached to those labels, they may not even want to know you. Your children might watch a lot of prison documentaries on television, with all the interviews of mean-looking convicts with shaved heads, scary tattoos, and big muscles. It doesn't help that Mom tells them you are a dangerous criminal and that you "done her wrong." Can you blame your kids if they are afraid of you and want to protect her at all costs?

If your former spouse is uncooperative, be careful. She can call your parole officer (PO), make up some story, and you get a one-way ticket back to the joint. You are an ex-convict on parole; do not assume you will be welcomed back by your family with open arms. People will have personal reasons (oftentimes irrational by your standards) why they do or do not want to see you.

If you have reason to believe that your ex-spouse is hostile toward you, ask your PO, a minister, or a good friend to come with you the first time you visit your kids. You need them to serve as a witness, just in case somebody decides to call the police.

You may want to inform your PO if you plan on visiting your ex-wife or ex-husband or trying to reestablish relationships with your children. This is for your protection, especially if you already know your ex-spouse will be hostile or uncooperative. POs do not like surprises.

Depending on how long you were behind bars, and what your ex-spouse has said to your children about you, she may not want to even see you. This is especially true if you did time in federal prison or a large state penitentiary like in Texas or California, where it's likely you were shipped to some distant institution and received few or no family visits.

So think about the last time you saw your children, how old they are now, and what is best for them. You may need to wait until they are older to form a deeper connection with them. Perhaps by then they will be able to understand your situation.

If your kids are not in the custody of your ex-spouse, they could be under the care of your mother, aunt, sister, or brother. They might also be in a foster home, juvenile detention center, mental health facility, orphanage, group home, or even be adopted. Wherever your children are, find them. As their biological parent, this is your first duty.

They need to see you, even if they think they do not want to know you. They may decide later that they need you in their lives. Do what you can to encourage this type of thinking. Even if your kids don't show it at the time, telling them that you love them and want them in your life will mean a lot to them.

## Relationships with Your Parents and Siblings

Hopefully, your birth family welcomes your return home. This is the family who brought you into this world, missed your presence on birthdays, anniversaries, and holidays, and visited you in jail or prison when they could.

You might want to see them first before going to look for your ex-wife and children. Not only do you love your mom and dad, but they may have information concerning your wife and children. It is possible that they have kept in contact with your ex-spouse and kids while you were incarcerated.

Then again, they may have given up on you long ago. If they did, it will take an incredible amount of courage, persistence, and patience on your part to try to reconnect with your family.

While you were in prison, your family changed. Your mom or dad, uncle or aunt, sister or brother may have passed away. You may not even know when or how. Maybe your family decided not to tell you while you were in custody because they knew you would not be allowed to attend the funeral and they didn't want to upset you any more than necessary. To help deal with your grief and guilt for not being by their side when they died, go to the cemetery or mausoleum and pay your respects.

If one or both of your parents are still alive, plan to spend some time with them. They need to see you free and tell you things they have been waiting years to say. You know your mom and dad have been discussing your problems for years. They will have something to say, like "I told you so" or "I wish you listened to your old man." Try to listen politely without arguing or defending yourself. Try not to cast blame or point the finger. And then politely ask what you can do for them. They may just be relieved to know you are alive and free again.

If you have sisters and brothers, go see them; ask them what has happened in their lives while you were away. Do what you can to be a good brother, sister, uncle, or aunt.

## Getting Back Custody of Your Children

You need to do what is best for your children. This is not always easy to determine. At the very least you know you need a job, a way to pay the bills, and a place to live that is appropriate for them in case you get permission to have them spend the night. This will take some time and considerable effort.

## Don't Rush Into Anything

If you have a low-paying job, or are attending college, you may need to wait. While you are on parole, you could be returned to a correctional facility with little notice. And no one wants this to happen when their children are in their custody. Be patient; it may take a few years to recover from jail or prison and get back on your feet.

Taking custody of kids while you are on parole is very risky. In fact, having children in your house may even add to the risk. As we discussed previously, your children may be resentful of you. If one of them were to call your PO and complain about you, or even say you were drinking beer, or violating curfew, you could be arrested and returned to prison. We have even heard of cases where parolees were violated because their teenage children were arrested for drugs, underage drinking, or stealing a car.

If your goal is to get full or joint custody of your children, then you need a good job, a nice place to live, and some confidence that you will be able to successfully complete parole. Family courts are not eager to give any kind of custody of dependent kids to parolees. At the very least you will have to think carefully about what is best for your children now and in their future.

Of course, some ex-convicts, particularly women, are given their children as soon as they get out of jail or prison. Your extended family may be more than happy to give you immediate custody. Maybe they are tired of caring for your kids. Sometimes social workers pressure formerly incarcerated moms to assume responsibility for their children before it is even practical.

In some situations, it may be more difficult to retrieve the kids from the bureaucratic grasp of human service agencies, foster care, or group homes. Some agencies are less than eager to return children to ex-convict parents. Depending upon your criminal record, the law may not even allow them to return your kids to you. For example, if you were convicted of domestic assault or a sex offense, you might not be allowed custody of your children. You may need to meet with the human service agency many times, provide evidence that you can support your children, and get a court order before they will be returned to you.

You need to think long and hard about what kind of life your children had *before* you went to prison. Will they be better off with you or in someone else's care now? The kids' needs—and not yours—must be put first. What they need most is a stable and loving home.

## Document Everything

When making contact with your children for the first time, our best advice is to write, e-mail, or call the custodial parent or institution, introduce yourself, and ask about your children. Inquire as to what you need to do to get permission to see them. Be sure your inquiries are polite, and express your concern for your children's welfare. Keep copies of your letters or e-mails and the replies you receive in a safe place like a safety deposit box.

Buy a legal pad or notebook. At the very top of each page write the name of the person you called, the phone number, and the date. Document your questions as well as their responses. Try to be as accurate as you can transcribing what was said. Do not audiotape phone calls, unless you have carefully checked the prevailing law in your state.

In order to get custody or visitation rights, you might need to build a record of contact or correspondence. Family court judges like to see records when they decide custody and visitation rights. You may need to present this in a future court hearing, where it may help prove that you care about your children and are and have always been interested in restoration of your parental rights.

Some women who've filed for divorce may still regard you as the kids' father. Other women may just want to collect child support payments, while they obstruct your efforts to see your children. To compound the problem, your children may harbor considerable resentment of the "How could you do this to me?" variety, which will not be easily overcome. Your ex-husband or wife or girlfriend may feed their resentment, and even encourage hostility toward you. Your wife may have been telling nasty stories about you to the children.

Eventually, your kids, perhaps out of curiosity, will want to hear the rest of the story. When they ask, try to avoid criticizing their mother. Stick to the facts without assigning blame. If they are old enough, just tell them the simple truth.

You need to be incredibly patient negotiating the potentially rough waters in this situation. No matter the circumstances, and how you are perceived at first, you must remind your children that you love them. Over and over, they need to hear you say, "I love you."

## Sex: How Are Joe and Jill Making Out?

Joe and Jill have been through a lot. They get out of prison to find that the world went on without them. Returning home, they are older and most likely single and alone.

### Easing Back Into Things

After years in the joint, you have a lot of unmet emotional and sexual needs. Most inmates go sexually dormant in prison. They typically live like a priest or a nun without sex. Maybe your spouse or girlfriend wants you back, and you simply start over where you left off. More than likely she won't take your phone calls, or she hangs up when she hears your voice on the other end of the line.

If you go to a bar, you might decide to pick up the first person who smiles at you. This can work for a while. But remember to practice safe sex. Use a condom and/or other form of birth control to prevent sexually transmitted diseases and unplanned pregnancies. Your life is already difficult enough without these additional complications.

## Joe on the Make

After Joe completes his stay at the halfway house and is formally on parole, he rents a modest apartment. He was smart enough to look for a place in a quiet neighborhood where people have jobs and don't tolerate a lot of street crime. Neighbors sweep their porches, tend their small lawns, and go to tavern fish fries on Friday nights. Maybe they hang out in barbershops or beauty parlors where they discuss the news or share neighborhood gossip. This is one of those communities where people congregate in corner bars to watch ballgames, eat, or see their friends. Joe is able to afford the rent, pay child support, see his children once a month, and have a few dollars left for beer. Things are pretty good.

As time passes, Joe starts wishing he had someone to share his time with, if not for love, then at least for sex.

He avoids the seedy biker bars, like where he met his ex-wife. Nightclubbing coke-head biker ladies are out, unless they have reformed, left the fast lane, given up the cocaine, and slowed down to Joe's speed. Older now, he can't handle the loud music and young crowd. So, he checks out the corner bars at lunch, goes back on Friday night to have dinner, and eventually becomes a regular. Joe is looking to meet a nice lady who will accept him for who he is.

## Jill Searches for Mr. Right

Like a lot of women, Jill has made her mistakes with men. It took her years to realize that while men want sex, women get babies, and none of this necessarily adds up to love.

Older and wiser now, Jill has enough to do just being a mother, without taking on the additional responsibility of a man who just does not seem to want to grow up. Still, she doesn't think she can survive economically on her own.

Jill came home to a world that suddenly got more expensive. She can't believe the price of milk, meat, fruit, and gas. She has a job that barely covers essentials, with nothing left over for childcare. How can she work and care for her children all by herself? How does she make it on just one paycheck in a two-paycheck world? She will have to find somebody to share housing expenses. This could be a man, woman, or, more than likely, her mother or sisters.

Jill would like to meet a steady guy, without a bad temper, who can keep a job and help pay the bills. Alternatively, she will settle for a responsible roommate. No more sweet, handsome men with expensive clothes and flashy cars who come and go as they please. No sir, she wants a guy who wants love first and sex later.

Of course he will have to be good to her children. She knows it takes a special guy to accept another man's kids as his own. This takes time. At the very least he has to be able to spend time as a family, and never yell at or hit her children. Maybe then he will come to see them as his own.

Jill won't need to search for a man at a bar or nightclub. Still relatively young and attractive, they will come to her on their own. Maybe after all the mistakes in her life, she will exercise better judgment now. Hopefully she will find her prince charming. Jill is looking for love that does not leave after sex. She wants a man who will help her make a life beyond the bedroom.

## Looking for Love

Coming out of prison, straight and sober, you should choose social settings where people enjoy each other's company without chemical assistance. Avoid hooking up with the first attractive member of the opposite sex you meet at an Alcoholics Anonymous (AA) or

Narcotics Anonymous (NA) meeting, or sitting next to you in the waiting room at the parole office.

There are other places to meet nice men and women. We suggest you explore community events and organizations. For example, many universities, community colleges, libraries, and churches hold educational and social events open to the public. You might take some adult education courses at the local community college, YMCA, or local community center where you may meet some appropriate friends and even potential partners.

Many volunteer groups actively recruit new members. Some of these organizations are involved in political, social, community, or religious services that draw large numbers of single men and women. If you live in a big city, we suggest you check out prison-reform organizations. Just be careful, because ex-convicts are everywhere. You will meet many at AA, NA, or correctional-reform organization meetings. You just need to remember that association with "known felons" can be interpreted as a parole violation.

Many convicts spent time working out in prison, lifting weights, or jogging, and might want to continue these activities when they get released. You may meet men and women at recreational centers or through sports clubs. Just make sure they are not already married. You have enough of your own problems; you don't need to complicate your life by dating people who are already hitched. Besides, you don't want to contribute to more broken homes. Keep in mind that some people don't wear their wedding rings in swimming pools.

It's okay if you are a little shy. You should be. After all, you need to be careful, considering how long it really takes to get to know somebody new. You don't want to hook up with a woman who just needs you to support her children, mow her lawn, fix her car, or repair her home. Don't be a fool for a smile and a soft bed. After a couple of nights in the sack you move in and assume responsibility for all her problems.

We have seen this happen once too often. The convict returns home, has a small paycheck, and then meets a pretty lady with a good cover story but big monthly bills. He moves in with this woman, who also has her own kids and lots of unmet needs. He wants to prove he's a man again, so he puts his educational and career plans on hold and immediately assumes her obligations.

With his meager income, he can't help her enough. Wanting to play hero, he goes back to his hustle to make more money on the side. Maybe he slings a little dope, or turns a profit with stolen merchandise. The next thing you know, he's going back to jail or prison on a new conviction, and she's found another live-in lover. You can't make up for your years inside in one night with the first person who comes your way, so don't even try.

# Chapter 10

## The Devil You Know: Avoiding Alcohol, Drugs, Weapons, and Violence

Lots of things can get an ex-convict violated. Many of them we mentioned elsewhere in this book, including three of the most dangerous temptations: possession and use of alcohol, illegal drugs, and weapons. Moreover, formerly incarcerated people must be very careful not to engage in violence in order to solve their disputes or even express their pent-up depression or rage.

## Public Enemy #1: Alcohol Abuse

Ask any police officer, nurse, or doctor: alcohol abuse is the most serious social problem in this country. In every small town and big city in America, the jails are filled with drunks. They are arrested for driving while impaired, getting into drunken bar brawls, and engaging in violent family quarrels. After a series of arrests they often lose their jobs, friends, and then their families. Eventually they live in rented rooms, homeless shelters, or makeshift shelters that they built under bridges or in urban parks. Some will die of liver damage or related diseases. Others are actually saved by jails and prisons, where they get treatment and kick the habit.

A lot of people don't realize they are alcoholics until they are arrested and sent to jail. On the street they had money and easy access to beer, wine, and liquor. Maybe in the free world they were functional alcoholics with a family and a job. They had a few drinks or beers every day, maybe at lunch, after work, or before bed. These individuals knew they had a problem, but they could manage until they were locked up.

## Alcohol and Parole Supervision

Failing drug or alcohol tests is the number-one reason why paroles are returned to jail or prison.

Many ex-convicts think they kicked their habit in the joint, only to return home and get perpetually drunk or addicted again. Very few ex-cons realize that they maintained their sobriety and stayed clean while locked up because their access to booze and dope was restricted. When they return home to the free world of bars and buddies with dope, it's all too easy to get sucked back into the old addictions.

In general, most federal parolees are allowed to consume alcoholic beverages unless specifically ordered not to by a judge or parole officer. But federal parolees do not realize that the federal government continues close surveillance of their activities while on parole. This may include wiretaps—bugging their homes, cars, and offices—and secret audits of their financial assets. If the parolee buys a new car or fancy home, opens a business, or transfers large sums of money, the feds may come down with new indictments. Federal parole officers, cooperating with FBI and DEA agents, monitor parolees for violations of federal laws—for example, Continuing Criminal Enterprises (CCE), or Racketeer Influenced and Corrupt Organizations (RICO), all of which carry very heavy sentences.

The point is that a federal parole officer usually does not care if a parolee drinks alcohol or uses illegal drugs. The feds are not interested in busting a mafia boss or drug cartel banker for drinking in a bar or smoking a joint. As a matter of fact, the feds love how some people talk and brag about their criminal activities when they are drunk or high. They might actually *prefer* you drunk as a skunk or buying a Rolls Royce for your mistress, so they can catch you talking about your more serious crimes. Then they can return you to the federal penitentiary on a life sentence.

In contrast, most states *do not* allow any people on probation or parole to drink beer, wine, or spirits. This is probably because many people in county jails or state prisons were intoxicated when they committed the crimes that landed them in the slammer.

These individuals may have chronic problems with alcohol consumption. They may commit crimes just to get money to pay for drugs or booze. For example, a lot of people convicted of burglary, assault, vandalism, or disorderly conduct were drunk at the time of their infraction. Of course, driving under the influence can also lead to a stretch in state prison.

Given the fact that many people coming out of county jail or state prison have a long history of heavy drinking, parole officers have good reason to prohibit parolee use of alcohol. Besides, state probation and parole officers know that alcohol consumption is often related to petty crimes, common burglary and theft, assault, drunk driving, and domestic violence. They also understand that many of their clients are alcoholics and will return to their previous daily bad habits upon release from a correctional facility.

In fact, parole agents may search a parolee's home, and if they find one empty beer can, they have the right to arrest, violate, and return them to jail or prison. Remember, parole officers do not need search warrants. Large parole offices in big cities might have 20 to 30 parole officers, each with 50 to 100 clients in their caseload. Every week they prepare a list of parolees for home searches. These may be clients who have failed alcohol or drug screens, are suspected of dealing drugs again, or are being investigated for other crimes.

Many parole offices actually have "crash cars" they use for "search and destroy" missions. One or more parole officers dress in SWAT team gear, including shotgun, side arm, bullet-proof vest, and helmet. They drive the vehicle, usually an SUV, to a location where they meet their police escort. Then the convoy proceeds to each home. At each address the parole officers enter the house first with the police right behind. Upon finding any alcohol, they arrest the parolee and then continue the search, looking for evidence of new crimes. When they are finished, they transport him or her to jail.

Our advice to parolees who are restricted from drinking or having alcohol is to have no beer, wine, or spirits in your home or in your workplace desk or locker at any time. It does not matter who bought it or who consumes it. This means if you live with your parents, they have to box up their liquor cabinet and remove it from the premises. You can be violated for any alcoholic beverage in the house, garage, or even the garbage can outside.

We also suggest that ex-cons avoid inner-city neighborhoods with bars, liquor stores, and corner drug dealers. These are formidable temptations. Instead, choose a quiet residential neighborhood of homes and schools, where there are no billboards or bar signs advertising booze and beer.

## Alcoholics/Narcotics Anonymous

If you even suspect that you have an alcohol or drug problem, you should consider joining Alcoholics Anonymous and/or Narcotics Anonymous. These programs exist all over the world and have helped millions of people to get sober and stay that way. AA and NA are predicated on the idea that alcoholism and drug abuse are diseases that require treatment. Their 12-Step Program is a powerful tool for reordering your life.

Almost every prison has a daily AA meeting. These are usually organized by convicts and free-world volunteers. Maybe while incarcerated you attended an AA or NA meeting for amusement, entertainment, companionship, or distraction, or simply because you thought it would look good on your parole application. Then again, you may have learned about the serious business of people learning to overcome their addictions and thought it might help you, too.

At the meetings people bare their souls and talk about their addictions. They stand up one at a time and share how alcohol or drugs destroyed their lives. Attendees tell how they lost marriages, kids, jobs, and self-respect. You realize this disease is a common, learned behavior, and is difficult to overcome. It takes courage and resolve to confess your problems in a group meeting, especially in prison.

Some convicts attend AA/NA meetings for many years behind bars. Maybe they did the same on the street before coming to prison. As regulars, they make friends with the volunteers. The volunteers may even agree to serve as a mentor. Sometimes these relationships become lifelong friendships. When men or women get out of the joint, their mentors may help them find a place to live, or even a job.

One of the core ideas behind AA/NA is that people must accept the fact that they are alcoholics/addicts. They need to stop blaming others for their situation, and take personal responsibility. They must also understand that changing their self-defeating behavior like alcohol and drug dependency may also mean changing situations that acted as triggers for their addiction. This can include associating with certain people, places, and things.

Usually, AA/NA meetings are held one day a week at each location, such as a church, temple, community center, library, college, or university. An alcoholic might attend meetings every day or evening at different locations. Usually they have a list of locations with days and times. When they travel to another town or city, they can consult the phone book and call AA/NA, or go online to find a meeting.

AA/NA is a community that most people do not know about until they attend. You will find the AA/NA groups everywhere across the country. We call it a parallel community of people because it exists side by side with the larger community of sober adults. The purpose of the AA/NA community is to help people find sobriety or a drug-free lifestyle.

Some of these meetings are small, with just a few people. Other meetings may have hundreds of people, with gifted speakers, films, and even free food. At these gatherings you meet all kinds of people, from many walks of life. There may even be business owners, recovering alcoholics themselves, who offer employment to AA/NA members. After meetings people congregate at restaurants where they drink coffee or soda and continue mentoring.

# Illegal Drugs

We live in a society where people have been led to believe that illegal drugs are the cause of every crime imaginable. Every day, the news and mass media feature stories reinforcing the idea that drug-crazy people are robbing, stealing, and assaulting the public at every turn.

The "war on drugs" has provided the criminal justice system with huge amounts of federal and state tax money to hire law enforcement, appoint judges, and build new jails and prisons. Unfortunately, this tax money came from your paychecks and pockets. Too bad the money was not spent on better schools, mass transit, and economic development that would create new jobs.

## Urine Testing

To get a job these days, or even to keep it, many Americans must submit to drug testing. This is especially true for entry-level positions in blue- and pink-collar occupations. If you just got out of jail or prison and are applying for jobs, you should expect to be piss tested at fast-food restaurants, retail stores, and assembly plants. If your Pre-Sentence Investigation, rap sheet, or prison file indicates you have ever used drugs, you can expect to be tested at the parole office. While most employers absorb the costs, the parole office will make you pay for every drug screen.

You may have also heard that there is an entire industry devoted to selling testing services to employers and criminal justice agencies. Drug testing has become big business. There are also companies that sell advice and chemicals that supposedly help people beat drug testing. The result has been a high-tech race to design equipment and procedures that can help you fool or foil the tests. Add to this an entire litany of urban mythology about ways to use drugs and defeat the tests.

Here's the best way to beat a urine test: avoid using illegal drugs. This is the only way to really be safe from drug-test parole violations. Playing Russian roulette with drug tests is a game you will eventually lose.

People will tell you they bought some magic potion at a head shop, from a catalogue, or on the Internet to help them mask drug use. The products are sold under many names, including Instant Clean, Test Klear, Urine Luck, Mary Jane Super Clean, Stealth, or Golden Seal. Many other products are also on the market; most of them are some combination of soap, acid, or other chemicals designed to cover or disguise illegal drug use.

A lot of people who use these products think they actually worked for them. Who knows: maybe some of these potions do work. The problem is that although someone pissed in a specimen bottle, she doesn't know what happened to the sample after that. Maybe that particular sample never actually got tested because some parole offices only send a small number of urine samples to labs to be analyzed.

Other offices have their own on-site testing machines. Sometimes these devices are out of order or there aren't enough staff to test all the samples. The bottom line is that sooner or later your urine will be tested and the products detected.

Ex-cons also try to beat drug tests by diluting the sample. Parole staff people are aware of this trick, and so they watch you piss in the bottle. There's usually no sink in the room, and the toilet water is tinted. Even if you manage to get over these obstacles and add water to your sample, new testing procedures will uncover and flag the sample as diluted. You can be violated for attempting to mask or dilute a urine sample, even if the authorities don't find traces of illegal drugs.

We have also heard stories about people who attempt to substitute clean urine from somebody else. We remember talking to one guy who constructed a rudimentary contraption out of medical and aquarium supplies. This included a plastic bag he wore under his armpit, flexible plastic tubing that he duct-taped down the side of his body, hidden inside his shirt, to his penis, and a valve he opened for fake peeing. He would fill the bag with another person's "clean" urine, go to the parole office, wait to be escorted into the bathroom to piss, and then while he was observed, he would open the valve and fill the bottle with "legal" piss. His elaborate system worked for a while, and he got away with the scheme for a few months. Then one day while sitting in the waiting room at the parole office the bag broke and leaked out all over his shirt. He was immediately arrested and dragged off to jail.

The most tried-and-true method of defeating drug testing is to simply drink a lot of water to flush your system. Some people suggest apple juice or vinegar, but be careful, as drinking large quantities of vinegar can cause liver damage. Again, you don't know what happens to your sample in any given test. You get away with it for a while only because your sample wasn't tested. Besides, we know that parole offices and testing labs with the latest equipment can detect drugs in your urine no matter how much it is masked, diluted, or flushed.

So what do you do if you have taken drugs or drunk alcohol and you have to take a urine test? We suggest being completely honest with your parole officer. The vast majority of them are more concerned about your ability to tell the truth than your ability to stay clean. Depending upon your relationship with your PO, you might be better off admitting to your dope use than trying to fool the test. The PO may appreciate your sincerity. He might even accept that you are dirty and give you another chance. On the other hand, if you fail the drug test, and your sample was flagged as adulterated or he thinks you tried to mask the dope, he could get mad at you, pull your probation or parole, and send you to jail.

Finally, some parole offices use hair testing and saliva or oral drug screens. They have all the latest technology available, although they might not display it in the parole office. If they really want to nail you for illegal drug use, they can test your pee, hair, and spit all on the same day. There is no way you can win the game.

## Drug Use

Returning to the streets to party with or deal in illegal drugs is dangerous. Besides, while you were in jail or prison your street smarts were probably dumbed down. You may have lost your ability to judge your surroundings. You no longer know the cast of characters who work in the neighborhood. If you return to slinging dope or even hanging with those who do, you will only draw attention, and probably get others arrested along with yourself.

If you really need chemical help, go to a free medical clinic and talk to a doctor about getting a prescription. Learn what most middle-class Americans take for granted: the best dope is legal. Just take your prescription to the drug store. And remember to keep a record of your legal doctor prescriptions in case they register on a drug screen test.

# Weapons

As a convicted felon, you are not allowed to own or possess firearms or other weapons. You cannot own a pistol, rifle, or shotgun. As a matter of fact, you cannot even live in a house where other residents own guns.

While you are "on paper"—meaning probation, parole, or community custody—a parole officer (PO) can enter your home without a warrant at any time, without any apparent reason or appointment. She can come in the middle of the night, alone or with police backup. The PO does not want to be greeted by a person with a weapon.

Therefore, parolees should make absolutely sure that all weapons, including firearms, even inoperative or ornamental ones, are removed from the premises. For good measure, if you or the residents in your house are part-time collectors, all swords, martial arts weapons, hunting knifes, mace, tasers, and stun guns should also be stored at another location.

Thousands of felons catch new criminal cases because they don't understand that, as a felon, they cannot own or even be near firearms. The fact that the gun is owned by another person will not protect you from arrest and conviction.

Never allow yourself to sleep in a house or ride in a vehicle where a firearm or weapon is kept, regardless of ownership. And if these words of advice seem a little paranoid, don't forget that almost anything can be considered by law enforcement to be a weapon, including a pen, pencil, or a car.

## Felony Firearm Laws

As a convicted felon, you are subject to both state and federal laws concerning the purchase, ownership, possession, sale, and use of a firearm. You should consult both state and federal laws before buying a shotgun, rifle, or handgun. The laws are very complex, and can carry serious sanctions, including long mandatory prison sentences.

For example, upon indictment for a felony, even before trial or conviction, you are prohibited from purchasing or possessing a firearm. Upon arrest or indictment, immediately remove all firearms from your residence. We advise you to take them to a gun store, sell them, and get a receipt.

Why? Let's say you are under indictment; if law enforcement wants to hassle you, they may come to your house with a search warrant to look for guns. You do not want them tossing your house looking for weapons. If you want to spare yourself the inconvenience, meet them at the door and give them the receipts you received at the gun store.

It can also be illegal in some states to possess firearms while serving a sentence for a misdemeanor or domestic assault conviction. If you are convicted of disorderly conduct, or simple assault, you may not be allowed to possess firearms while on probation. Once you have served the prescribed misdemeanor sentence, your right to bear arms is typically restored.

Federal law prohibits possession of firearms for any felony, even if the sentence is suspended. This means if the sentence is more than one year (a felony), despite the fact you were given probation and never spent a day in jail or prison, then you are a felon and can never again buy, own, sell, or use a firearm.

If your state or federal conviction has been set aside, overturned, pardoned, expunged, or exonerated, you still need to consult the law or a good lawyer before you assume it is safe to go deer or duck hunting. Do not assume that because some rights—such as voting or the right to hold elected office—have been restored, you are free to purchase or own a gun. By the way, you should know that while states may restore voting privileges, federal law governs the restoration of the right to bear arms. If you have a federal felony conviction, you need a Presidential Pardon in order to legally possess or use a firearm again.

Federal law prohibits more than just felons from possessing firearms. A quick look at United States Code is a real eye opener. According to USC TITLE 18, PART I, CHAPTER 44, § 922, it is a federal crime for any person to possess a firearm (1) who "has been convicted in any court of a crime punishable by imprisonment for a term exceeding one year"; (2) who "is a fugitive from justice"; (3) who "is an unlawful user of or addicted to any controlled substance"; (4) who "has been adjudicated as a mental defective or who has been committed to a mental institution"; (5) who, "being an alien, is illegally or unlawfully in the United States"; (6) who "has been discharged from the Armed Forces under dishonorable conditions"; (7) who, "having been a citizen of the United States, has renounced his citizenship"; (8) who is "subject to a court order that restrains such person from harassing, stalking, or threatening an intimate partner of such person or child of such intimate partner or person, or engaging in other conduct that would place an intimate partner in reasonable fear of bodily injury to the partner or child"; and (9) who "has been convicted in any court of a misdemeanor crime of domestic violence." Please consult the USC Title 18 and a lawyer for specific language, legal interpretation, and the most up-to-date court decisions.

We hasten to add that the maximum penalty for being a felon in possession of a firearm is 10 years behind bars and a $250,000 fine. This is a mandatory sentence, usually added on top of other convictions. For example, a person might be convicted of burglary, plea bargain for a sentence in state court, and then be remanded to federal court where he is convicted of a weapons charge and receives an additional 10 years. In many jurisdictions, a defendant convicted on a misdemeanor drug conviction receives a few months for the dope and then 10 years for the gun.

## Violence

Parole officers are experts at testing their clients for anger or violent reactions. They will push your buttons when you report to their office, converse with you on the phone, or visit you at work or at home. On purpose, they might get you fired from your job, threaten you on the phone, or come to your home and make fun of you in front of your family.

The idea is to get you mad. The parole officer is checking you out. He might come to your home with a second officer. Then they sit at your kitchen table and joke about busting you while playing with handcuffs. They might insult you or your family. The PO might order you to assume "the position," face to the wall or lying on the floor, with your hands cuffed, while another agent searches every room in the house. All the time they are both watching your face and body language. They are testing you for anger.

It is their job to be suspicious, to pry, to provoke, and to ask questions about your personal life, behavior, and associations. They may disapprove of anything, including your appearance, friends, family, or the way you respond to questions.

No matter what they do, never show anger or let them get you mad. Stay cool, calm, and collected. After all, what can they do to you? Take you to jail? Big deal; you have been there before.

You must be very careful about how you relate to people at home and work. You can be returned to jail or prison on one verified report of violence or threat of violence. If your girlfriend or ex-wife calls the parole officer or police to say that you threatened her, you will more than likely go back to jail or prison. If your boss fires you, you must keep your cool and leave quietly. No matter what people say to you, or how shabbily you are treated, watch what you say and always walk away before you lose your temper.

Another common mistake is when an ex-convict starts thinking that she is just like everybody else, a free person with no criminal record. This is tempting fate. As a convicted felon, a person with a criminal and prison record, you are different—at best a semi-citizen, and at worst another usual suspect, or a person of interest to law enforcement. Being an ex-con, you know they wouldn't mind sticking you with another rap.

Keep in mind that, as the police can arrest and hold you with less evidence than the average citizen, the prosecutor can persuade a jury to convict with little effort, and the judge can sentence you to more time based on your previous convictions. So the first sentence is never really done; once you have one strike, the second is easier to get, and the courts love to hang you with the third, which in some states means a life sentence.

While on parole or community supervision, you may be ordered by the court or by your parole officer to attend Aggression Management Counseling programs. Often touted as a cure for violence-prone individuals, at these meetings you might learn (if you don't know already) to count to 10 before you lose your temper, to lower your voice and increase your distance from a person when holding a conversation, or to simply walk away from an argument.

Whatever is being taught as aggression management, do not complain or skip the meetings. Your lack of attendance, or even failing to pay attention in class, might be interpreted negatively by the judge or parole officer as noncooperation.

## Association with Known Felons

Another final, often-ignored condition of parole is not associating with "known felons." In many respects, this is code for not engaging in crime again. The problem with this requirement is that almost anywhere you go, you are bound to run into felons. For example, in cities like Washington, D.C., approximately one in every three African American males between the ages of 18 and 35 is under the supervision of the criminal justice system. In Baltimore, it is one in every four. Similar statistics can be cited for most metropolitan areas in the country. The point is, you will find felons everywhere.

There are millions of people on probation or parole, walking city streets and riding the transit systems. Thus, by simply going about your daily life, more than likely you are going to run into felons. There is no way of getting around this fact.

You will meet felons at AA or NA meetings, at Anger Management group meetings you are ordered to attend, or standing in line at job service or the unemployment office. The room will be filled with former prisoners, some of them just out of the penitentiary, others who did a few months in the county jail, and many more who completed their sentences years ago.

In prison, a person is a prisoner or convict. When he gets out of prison and completes his entire sentence, he is a formerly incarcerated person, or ex-convict. In comparison, "once a felon, always a felon," unless the conviction has been pardoned or exonerated. There are very few ex-felons.

Some people don't even know they are felons. A person can be a felon without ever spending any time in jail or prison, so she was never a convict or an ex-convict. She was convicted of a felony, but served the sentence on probation. In the United States, there are many more felons than convicts or ex-convicts. Millions of convicted felons have never served time in prison.

Our best advice is to just be careful with whom you make friends, bring home, decide is your new buddy, or even shack up with. Your new love may be a known felon and a one-way ticket back to prison. Don't be surprised if your parole officer runs a criminal background check on your new girlfriend or boyfriend. As smarmy as this may sound, we suggest you access online criminal background databases. At the very least, you need to know his or her criminal record before you make the introduction to your parole officer.

In general, if you report to the parole office as ordered and don't get caught up with booze, dope, guns, or violence, you have a chance of successfully completing community supervision. You may perceive the subtleties as unfair, but they are the rules, and you must follow them or risk being sent back to the joint.

# Chapter 11

## The Holy Trinity: Money, Debt, and Business

When you go to jail or prison, everything you leave behind at home is up for grabs. Some people get locked up when they are still young adults and have relatively little assets to lose. Older adults may be married with children, a home, accumulated property, and investments such as retirement funds. These people may suffer losses they will never recover from.

Most people can hang on to their family and property through brief periods in jail or prison. The family may survive intact a few days, weeks, or months while you are in the joint. It is a very different story when a judge hands down a prison sentence of even just a few years. Families don't understand that inmates rarely serve their entire sentences behind bars. They hear the judge say 5 or 10 years and start thinking about life without you.

Some spouses and children spend many years anticipating the windfall they may receive when parents or close relatives pass away and leave them a hefty inheritance. So it should not be surprising that some family members may actually think about your imprisonment in the same way. Few marriages are strong enough to endure the incarceration of a spouse. Love has very little to do with it. Your spouse will have to find some way to pay the rent or mortgage while you are in prison.

Incarceration is a lot like death except there is no funeral or body to bury. Upon being convicted of a crime, a person just disappears into the vast unknown of distant penal institutions. Somebody gets your clothes, furniture, computer, and eventually your collection of CDs and DVDs. Your best friend might assume ownership of your car or business.

Meanwhile, your wife sells the house, takes back her unmarried name, and runs off to Florida with your lawyer. Adding insult to injury, your young children are raised to think he is their father. All this happens without your knowledge or approval, while you fight for your life in the penitentiary. There is very little you can do to stop it.

When you went to jail or prison, you may have had little time to secure your property and financial assets. Some felons are lucky enough to be out on bail awaiting notification of a day to self-surrender. Judges may even give a convicted defendant a few days or weeks to secure his personal property and make arrangements to protect his financial assets. Ideally, a single adult might have time to sell his home and car, store his furniture, and move his investments into insured saving accounts. A spouse or parent may have additional arrangements to make for children. The problem is most judges couldn't care less about you or your need to get your affairs in order before you go to prison.

Unfortunately, many people are not granted bail or time out of jail to attend to personal matters. Even if they initially had bail, once a person confesses, plea bargains, or is convicted at trial, she is usually locked in jail. This is because some people are tempted to take off, and perhaps even leave the country. They are taken from the courtroom to a jail cell and then straight to state or federal prison.

After a few years behind bars, chances are that most of what you owned has evaporated into thin air. It was appropriated or stolen by friends, given away, or confiscated by the government, lawyers, and/or your family. You get out of prison with the clothes on your back, a cardboard box, and a few dollars. Returning to the community, you realize that in addition to finding a place to live, a job to support yourself, and rebuilding your family and social life, you have debts you must pay.

# Money

Very few prisoners manage to save money while working jobs behind bars. Convict pay scales are extremely low. Most inmates work for less than 25 cents an hour. This comes to $10 a week or approximately $500 a year.

A few convicts may have prison factory or inmate clerk jobs that pay up to a dollar an hour. Top pay behind bars might be $200 a month. Assuming he needs to spend $100 a month on canteen or commissary (e.g., food, stamps, phone, toiletries), the inmate might be able to save $1,000 a year.

Occasionally, a few men and women will exit prison with a few thousand dollars they have managed to save after many years of incarceration. But this is the exception rather than the rule. These former convicts will use the money they saved in prison to pay their way once they are home in the community. But it won't get them far.

## Professional Criminals

Some criminals are financially smart. They plan for a rainy day. They realize that crime is a dangerous game where they have to anticipate getting caught. For example, some professional criminals (such as bank robbers, jewel thieves, members of drug cartels, or the mafia) manage to hide some portion of their illegal profits before they are incarcerated. Anticipating they will have to do a few years in stir (in jail or prison) for the state or Uncle Sam (federal time), they bury the loot, or stash it in a bank account or safety deposit box under a different name.

Typically, they learn to bury cash underground, in some quiet place where they can dig it up later. In many ways, jewel thieves are probably the most adept at hiding loot. They usually fence some of their take and hide the rest for a rainy day. Their big advantage is that gemstones are small, easy to hide, and impervious to wet ground.

If members of large-scale international criminal organizations prove they are "stand-up" guys and do the time without trading in their colleagues, they can expect to receive considerable assistance when they return home. When foreign drug-cartel members get out of federal prison they are temporary locked in Immigration and Customs Enforcement (ICE) prisons. Then they are deported home to Colombia, Mexico, or some Caribbean island. Upon arrival, depending upon how much power the drug cartel retains in their home country, they might be imprisoned again, or retire in style.

In a similar way, the American Mafia may train its members to plan for the day they get released. As young men growing up, they had fathers and grandfathers in the same organizations. They had many opportunities to invest in family enterprises, like bars, restaurants, and retail stores.

Later in life, these investments might pay dividends or serve as pension plans. While on the street, many mafia soldiers paid their parents' mortgages. So years later when they get out of a correctional facility, after their parents have passed away, they will have a home to live in when they retire from crime. Of course, this scenario presupposes that the feds do not confiscate the businesses or home as illegal proceeds.

Finally, we should recall that prostitution is the "oldest profession." While there are no estimates of how many women or men are employed in this trade, we do know that there are many types of prostitutes. While not all prostitutes have a heart of gold, some high-class hookers do have a mind for business. There are even a few who save (or invest) their money preparing for a better future.

## Disorganized or Unaffiliated Criminals

In reality, most prisoners return home with very few assets, property, or even prospects. They had little before they were locked up, and have even less after they get out of prison. This is especially true of African, Hispanic, Latino, and Native American inmates. They come from and return to low-income communities, with high rates of unemployment and poverty. They have fewer employment opportunities and a more difficult time finding legal work than white parolees.

Minority ex-convicts are more likely than whites to give up on lawful employment, return to illegal work, and be violated and returned to prison. The combination of racial discrimination and community prejudice against felons can overwhelm the best of intentions.

Regardless of race or ethnicity, most men and women coming out of prison need to be educated in financial planning. Legal income is "slow" money, as compared to the "fast money" of illegal occupations. Ex-convicts need to learn how to budget their income and save money so that they don't return to crime. This means they have to learn how to use financial institutions to store and save the wages or salary they earn.

## Where to Store and Save Your Money

If you're like most ex-convicts, you probably keep the little money that you do have on you at all times or stashed in your apartment or house. But your money doesn't earn interest hidden in your mattress. You need to open a bank account and start earning interest on your money. A bank or credit union can provide you with free checking, a debit card, and interest on deposits.

Most financial planners suggest that you set aside a little money each month in a savings account. Ideally, you should have at least enough savings to pay your bills for three months. This provides you with a cushion, should you lose your job.

Once you have a bank account, you can have your paycheck direct-deposited into it. Your parole officer (PO) will also want to know that you have a relationship with a financial institution (and not because you once stuck it up). Having a bank account will also make it easier for you to keep monthly income reports for your PO. Your bank records provide you with a way to verify how you make and spend your money.

Most banks enable you to track your checking and savings accounts online. Accessing your account, you can balance your checkbook, transfer funds from one account to another, and check to see that your payroll check was deposited. You can also print out your account statements to demonstrate to your PO that you have a job, are paying your bills, and even are saving money for the future.

Your neighborhood bank is probably the safest place to keep your money. For your day-to-day convenience, you probably want a bank with many branches, ATM machines, and a drive-up window if you have a car. It's good to periodically visit your bank in person; this way you get to know the bank personnel who can help you with all sorts of financial advice now and in the future. Once you have been out of prison for a while, and have established yourself at work, you might want to apply for an auto loan or home mortgage. Banks are more likely to qualify you for a loan if you have maintained checking and savings accounts with them for a number of years.

## Climbing the Mountain of Debt

Unfortunately, many felons get released only to find themselves tied up in knots by old debt. Unless you have assets or a rich uncle, there may be little you can do to free yourself. Nevertheless, you have to try, even if it takes years to see the light of day.

The first few months after being released, in addition to finding a place to live, a job to support yourself, and rebuilding your family and social life, you need to pay attention to your debts, including money owed for credit cards, auto loans, mortgages, court fees and fines, court restitution, child support, student loans, taxes, and bankruptcy.

### Credit Card Debt

While in prison you did not receive all your mail. A lot of credit card companies know better than to waste postage mailing bills to correctional institutions. They know that if you are not dead, you are at least a deadbeat. Not even the post office will forward your mail to prison.

It's a different story once you get out of the halfway house and rent your own place. Then all your old plastic buddies find you at the same time. Your mailbox will fill up with credit card bills. Of course, prepare yourself for the real shock when you open the envelopes. All these credit cards bumped your interest rates. They might have raised your interest rate to 29.9 percent or higher. Depending upon your unpaid balance, interest rate, and your time in jail or prison, you may owe quite a lot of money. Unfortunately, the credit card companies plan on profiting big-time from your imprisonment.

## Auto Loans

If you went to jail, missed car payments, and your family was unable to make the payments for you, your ride is gone. More than likely the repo man came in the middle of the night and towed your car away. Many auto lots and banks make a handsome profit off repossessed vehicles.

In fact, those used car businesses that advertise easy credit are the worst. They pocket your down-payment and the installments you made, and hope you default. Miss one payment and they take back the car, wash and wax it, and return it their lot to sell it to someone else. Their favorite cars they sell many times. If you were in jail only a few months, and the "hook" never came, you may be able to save your car if you can pay up on the loan.

## Mortgages/Home Loans

Typically, lenders give you more time on a home than a car before they repossess it. Many factors influence how many months you may have before foreclosure and eviction, including the amount of your down-payment and accumulated equity, the housing market, and the bank or finance company you deal with.

If you paid 10 or 20 percent down when you bought the house, or have accumulated equity over the years, the bank may wait many months before initiating foreclosure proceedings. On the other hand, if you bought the home with nothing down, or with a "no documentation" loan, the bank could move for foreclosure in just a few months.

Usually, banks don't like foreclosures in slow real estate markets. This is because once the financial institution assumes legal possession of the home, they are responsible for the cost of utilities, repairs, insurance, and property taxes. These "holding costs" can be considerable in a market where homes sell slowly. In many ways the market dictates their decision.

If you are in jail for a few months, or even in prison for a few years, a bank may be open to negotiation. The important thing is to communicate with your bank about the loan and let them know about your situation.

## Court Fees and Fines

One of the primary functions of locking people up in city and county jails is to force them to pay what they owe to the courts. Many people go to jail because they fail to pay court fees, traffic fines, parking tickets, and child support.

In some jurisdictions, you are allowed to pay off what you owe the court by serving time in jail. For example, you owe $300 on parking or traffic fines and pay it off by 30 days in jail. You might also be assigned court fees for pleading guilty and for the number of hours your public defender worked on your case. (Most defendants are surprised to find that public defenders are not free.) These fees usually are no more than a few hundred or thousand dollars. If you're in prison or some other correctional facility, the fees will be deducted from your inmate pay. If you fail to make payments at the parole office, the court will garnish your paycheck. If you don't pay, the police will lock you up in jail.

## Court Restitution

You may also be required to make payments on court-ordered restitution. The order is usually part of your sentence, and may be much larger than fees and fines. Some individuals convicted of white-collar crimes have court-ordered restitution in the millions of dollars. Sometimes a judge will grant a banker or corporate executive probation and restitution, hoping they will repay what they stole. When they don't cough up the required cash, they go to prison.

Conversely, a judge might order a corporate criminal to a federal penitentiary, hoping to scare them into surrendering assets. The convicted felon gets to prison and meets the tough guys with tattoos. Terrified, he asks his lawyers to write to the judge asking for release to community custody in exchange for surrendering his assets.

The corporate criminal simply waits for his high-profile case to fade from media attention, and then his fancy lawyers go back to federal court. His legal counsel then surrenders his client's assets and submits a motion for modification of the original sentence. The legal writ might discuss the prisoner's age and medical issues, as well as surrender of assets.

The judge reduces the original sentence, providing the prisoner with immediate release from prison or the remainder of sentence to be served under community supervision. The order might cite time already served in jail and prison, advanced age or serious medical condition of prisoner, and substantial amount of restitution paid as reasons for reducing sentence.

When the wealthy corporate criminal gets out of prison, he sells his mansion and yacht to pay more of his court-ordered restitution and IRS penalties. He then serves the rest of his sentence on house arrest, wearing an electronic monitor on his ankle. If the crook is really rich, he might still have another mansion and Ferrari. In effect, he has bought his way out of prison.

Corporate criminals are not fools. Many plan for the day when they will get caught. For example, think about all those crooked bank executives who get paid millions of dollars a year. Many of them collect fat salaries presiding over the demise of their own companies. The banking executives use their golden parachutes to pay lawyers, restitution, and eventually their way out of long prison sentences.

In a similar way, a professional thief might plan to soften his fall. He will convert his stolen merchandize into cash or financial instruments. Then he leaves a big cash retainer with a criminal defense attorney, and hides the remainder under obscure corporate accounts in foreign banks as security. After a few years in prison, he will direct his attorney to deploy part of his savings as negotiation for his release from prison.

In America, some criminals do manage to buy their way out of prison. This is especially likely to happen if the victims of their crimes hope to recover their losses through court-ordered restitution. The fact is, the courts are more than willing to negotiate your sentence, even let you out of prison, in exchange for the return of the loot.

White-collar thieves aside, many small-time common criminals owe restitution to victims for damages or losses. In general, the court attempts to recover restitution to pay victims. For example, a person goes to prison for a DUI and having a car accident in which another person was seriously injured or killed. Another example is a person being convicted of sexual assault or aggravated assault where the victim is awarded court-ordered restitution, which may total in the tens of thousands of dollars. In these cases, the court will expect the defendant to serve the prison time and make a good-faith effort to pay off the restitution when he is released.

We need to make two important distinctions between fees, fines, and restitution:

- Fees and fines are owed directly to the court to cover costs associated with the conviction.

- Restitution is collected by the court (through jail, prison, or parole offices) to be paid to a third party, usually the victim.

In most jurisdictions, the court first applies your payments toward fees and fines. When these are paid, your next payments are paid toward restitution. Usually your PO will tell you when your fees and fines are all paid.

Second, in most jurisdictions a person can be returned to jail for failure to pay fees or fines, but not for failure to pay restitution. The reason is that fees and fines, like traffic ticket fines, are owed the court. This means the judge can issue a warrant for your arrest and then police can pick you up and return you to jail. The police will just come to the halfway house or parole office to find you.

In comparison, restitution is owed to a third party, like a debt. The most the court can do is garnish your wages and place liens on your car or home. If you have no job, car, or home, then there is little they can do, except make empty threats, to make you pay restitution. Of course, refusal to pay something on the restitution you owe will not win any popularity contests with your PO. You are better off paying your PO small payments for these sanctions, just to protect yourself from being violated for something else.

## Child Support

You probably never received a bill for child support, or made any payments while you were in prison. That doesn't mean the state has forgotten about you. While incarcerated, the amount owed continued to grow, probably with interest. Upon your release, your child support bill will be one of the many ugly surprises you will eventually receive in your mailbox.

Child support payments are awarded to the custodial party. This may be the father, mother, grandparent, foster parent, or agency caring for the child. In general, if the family court awarded one parent full custody, then she or he will get child support payments.

If the court decision is joint custody, there may be no child support.

In cases where a spouse has a highly paid profession, profitable business, high income, or inherited wealth, there may be court-ordered alimony. Child support and alimony can be anywhere from a few hundred to many thousands of dollars per month, depending upon the income and wealth of the noncustodial parent. A typical award might be $200 to $400 per month per child. Some states can award up to a fourth of a mother or father's gross monthly income.

We have met many men who have received court orders to pay child support for different kids conceived with different mothers. Their love life has complicated their economic survival. Their failure to pay child support may cause them to spend many years in and out of jail. Eventually, they may even be sent to prison for failure to appear in court. Over the years, their court record grows and makes it nearly impossible to get or keep a job. Employers don't like men who ignore orders to pay child support. This is a vicious cycle that is difficult, if not impossible, to break.

We usually think of men paying court-ordered child support payments to women. But the tables are turned when the woman goes to jail or prison. The family court reassigns custodial rights and orders her to make child support payments.

Our advice is to always respond (if not in person then in writing) in a timely fashion to the family court, social service agencies, and custodial parent. You may ask the family court to negotiate your bill, set aside fees and interest, or lower your monthly child support payments.

Go to court, bring any records you may have of payments made, contributions toward family expenses, your household bills, and your income or assets. Show the judge any canceled checks, credit card statements, and store receipts you may have for money you spent on your children. Then, tell the judge if you were unable to make payments while in prison. Ask the judge to reduce your past child support bill to reflect the fact. Request that future payments be based on the wages you now receive at your job.

If you fall behind on child support payments, you can be arrested, but usually only after a complaint is filed. This is why it is critically important that you are on the best of terms with the custodial parent. For example, if your ex-wife still likes you and knows that you have no means to pay child support, she might wait or hesitate to complain to the state. Just remember, as long as you owe a substantial amount of money on your child support account, you are at her mercy. This means you need to be considerate and resume payments as soon as you get on your feet.

## Student Loans

Student loans, regardless of whether they originated with the federal government, a state agency, or a private bank, continue to accumulate interest while you are in prison. They do not go away. If you fail to repay student loans, you face having your paycheck garnished and liens placed on your home. Once you default on a student loan, you cannot receive another until you repay the first loan.

If you've fallen behind on your student loans, contact your creditor. By law, you can request up to 24 months of forbearance on your outstanding loan balance. This means they still charge interest, but they cannot default the loan and your credit will not be negatively impacted.

Defaulting on any type of loan can seriously damage your credit score. This means you will pay higher interest rates for future consumer credit, like credit cards, auto loans, or home loans. A bad credit history can negatively impact your ability to get a job, get car insurance, or even get a checking account.

Finally, the federal government still maintains programs where you can earn full or partial forgiveness of your student loans. These have included working as a teacher, social worker, or nurse in disadvantaged or underserved communities. Military service after college graduation may also be used to forgive student loans. These programs may be of limited duration, change criteria, or lose funding. For the most up-to-date information, we suggest you consult relevant federal government websites.

## Taxes

Most prisoners don't file tax returns while behind bars. This is because most convicts don't have income to report, or tax refunds to expect, while in the joint. Besides, locked in jail or prison, even if you want to file your tax return, it is next to impossible without a free-world tax accountant or lawyer. You simply don't have access to the information you need to complete your tax return. Inmates are not allowed to keep financial records, or manage businesses, or even review business records while in prison. In some prisons, they can be locked in segregation for signing tax returns in the visiting room or discussing tax records on the telephone.

You are expected to resume filing taxes, including paying taxes for the past years where you had income in your name, when you get out of prison. The federal and state government should not penalize you, or charge interest, on the tax years you failed to file while incarcerated. However, they may still try to do so. You may need a tax accountant or lawyer to research the tax code and petition the IRS to remove penalties and interest.

The good news is that some colleges and universities and professional associations offer free tax advice. They even have volunteers who will help you complete your tax returns. They kick it into high gear around tax time (April 15th). You can also find free help with your tax returns at community centers and libraries. These services are especially intended for senior citizens, immigrants, and low-income individuals (which is probably you).

We should caution you that the complexity of the tax code, like ignorance of the law, is no protection. You will be expected to keep good tax records, file your tax returns on time, and keep tax returns in a fire-retardant file cabinet.

Every federal prison has a few nuts who are serving time for tax evasion. Forget all the nonsense you heard from these tax resisters. If these cons were as smart as they think they are, they wouldn't be in the penitentiary. If you become a tax protester, or teach or advise other people not to file tax returns, for whatever religious, political, or constitutional rationale you ascribe to, sooner or later you can expect a trip to federal prison.

## Bankruptcy

You may also find the Federal Bankruptcy laws provide some solace. Most lawyers advertise that they do not charge for initial consultation. They will give you a free appointment to explore your legal options. Generally, Federal Bankruptcy Laws may allow you to discharge certain debts or restructure debt, including credit cards and medical bills. You cannot discharge court-imposed fees and fines, child support payments, or student loans. However, you can discharge state and federal tax bills.

# Getting Out of Debt

In the case of legitimate debts, the best advice we can offer is to discuss the debt with your creditors and see what you can work out. Simply call them up, be polite and patient, and request their professional assistance. Ask for a reduction in interest and/or an extended payment plan. Do this before they proceed with garnishment of your wages or salary (i.e., take money directly out of your paycheck before it comes to you).

You may also find help at "free clinics," local libraries, universities, or community colleges. There are many community volunteers and college students providing services for indigent people. Call or visit community centers and educational institutions and ask about free debt counseling. Some university business and law schools offer legal advice for more complex problems.

When considering help, be very careful of debt consolidating firms or so-called credit counselors. These are the companies that advertise their services on late-night television or in the newspaper. Even if they advertise as nonprofits, these firms are in business to make money off you. Although they may sound like a logical solution and promise to have your best interests at heart, they are out to make money and prey upon people's ignorance.

Also, avoid borrowing money from storefront businesses that advertise fast money or payday loans. These are predatory lenders and you will end up paying exorbitant interest. Their goal is to charge big upfront fees and inflated interest, taking advantage of people who are in desperate need of cash. Depending upon the state and local jurisdiction, they can charge staggering rates of interest on consumer loans. While these businesses have been around for years in poor neighborhoods, they have multiplied and spread into middle-class communities in recent times.

Finally, beware of the many scam artists preying on homeowners. Some people use their homes like piggy banks, drawing down equity to pay for home repairs, renovations, or fancy vacations. Beware of mortgage brokers who want to refinance your mortgage. The recent failure of the housing market and bank closures has made it harder to get out of debt. People with no interest or variable-rate interest mortgages suddenly found that they could no longer afford to make their payments. Housing prices plummeted and people found themselves owing more on their houses than they were worth.

Avoid offers that arrive in the mail, by phone, or via e-mail without your invitation or solicitation. Most are too good to be true. These are typically scam artists pitching replacement windows, aluminum siding, cheap loans, and debt consolidation. They sell you something, collect their fees or sales commissions, and disappear, leaving you to read the fine print with a magnifying glass.

The best way to begin the process of getting out of debt is to first get a handle on what you owe. First, add up all outstanding debt, including credit cards, old utility bills, car loans, home loans, child support bills, medical bills, student loans, and unpaid taxes. Next, collect your credit reports, read them carefully, and compare them with the bills you have to pay. Make sure the reports accurately reflect your records.

Then, considering your debt and income, you need to learn to live within your means. After many years in jail or prison, you may be surprised by how expensive food, rent, and transportation appears. Here are some tricks to keep more money in your pocket. We suggest you make a monthly budget. Make one list of expected income. Make a second list of expected bills and anticipated expenditures. Then total each list and compare.

More than likely your expenses add up to more than your income. Look for ways to pare down your expenses. Cut out grocery store coupons in the newspaper. When you do go shopping for food and you place the items on the conveyer belt, make sure to reduce what you purchase by at least one item. Start a garden and grow some of your own food. Combine errands, walk to stores, or use public transportation to save gas. Most important, decide on items, services, or entertainment that you can live without. Just try to live on the take-home pay you receive.

Finally, chances are you are like millions of average Americans, working at a low-wage service job, or are out of work altogether. Remember, your biggest asset is you, your tenacity, and perhaps your ability to find creative solutions to problems that others find insurmountable. Your mission is to provide for yourself and your loved ones now and for the future.

Federal law entitles all Americans to a free copy of their credit reports each a year. You need to find out exactly what kind of debt the report lists and get in contact with the financial institutions as soon as possible. Be certain that the debts are actually yours. As you may have guessed, all sorts of wrong information can get posted to your account.

## Clearing or Expunging Your Criminal Record

Many ex-convicts would like to know if their criminal records can be cleared, sealed, or expunged. Unfortunately, it's nearly impossible to clear your record of convictions. This is true even when a person has been pardoned or exonerated. The fact that you completed your sentence does not mean your record can be cleared. The government maintains criminal history records for many purposes. The problem is that once information is entered into one database, it is shared with another database, and then it becomes almost impossible to completely erase.

The only criminal conviction records that can be sealed are those of minors. Depending on the jurisdiction and application, this age may vary, but it is usually 18, 19, or 20. Juvenile and family courts may seal cases to protect defendants. This is supposed to mean the case or criminal record cannot be used later in any adult court of law, but even then they are sometimes still used. Some civil cases that are settled outside of court can also be sealed.

Adult felony conviction records that have not been pardoned cannot be cleared, sealed, or expunged. State and federal computers will maintain these records until hell freezes over. You can complete your sentence, win the Medal of Honor and Noble Prize, die and be buried in Arlington National Cemetery, and your felony conviction record will still be public record, available to anyone. Only arrests that did not result in conviction can be cleared or expunged, and you will have to apply for the service, and there is no guarantee it will work. Don't believe anyone who tells you that he can clear your criminal record for a fee; he is trying to scam you.

The nationwide computerization of criminal conviction records did not begin until the 1980s. Before that time most criminal court and prison systems simply kept paper files. So if your criminal conviction is 20 or 30 years old, and you got out of prison back in the 1980s, it may not show up on computerized criminal background checks. If you went to prison in the 1980s, and got out of prison in the 1990s, then your criminal record is probably in the system.

Each state has its own system and standards for keeping criminal records. The quality of information varies. Files can be inaccurate and incomplete. If you have a common last name like Smith or Jones, Washington or Jefferson, or Garcia or Martinez, you may be easily victimized by mistaken identity. You may be confused with somebody else who has a very heavy criminal record.

## Starting Your Own Business

If you are on parole, the first year or two after getting out of prison you may need a job that pays wages or salary and provides a federal W2 Form. As we've noted previously, you need this to show your PO to verify how you earn your money.

Once you have completed some time on parole, however, you might think about starting a small part-time business. Take things slowly, and be sure to keep your day job while trying to get it up and running. Once your own business ramps up enough, you might be able to quit your regular job. After all, many people prefer to work for themselves.

Maybe you enjoy gardening, have some creative strengths, or have some mechanical ability. Can these interests lend themselves to a small business? Whatever you decide to try, you will need some careful thought, a business plan, and the motivation to work hard. You can begin your "home-grown" business with very little initial investment.

### Small-Scale Farming

If you have a green thumb, one option is to start a large garden and sell your extra produce for cash or barter for goods. Many amateur gardeners grow more food than they can use. Some people sell their surplus fruits and vegetables at roadside stands. Health-conscious consumers will even pay more for locally grown food, particularly if no pesticides or herbicides were applied.

To get a sense of the market, visit a few farmers' markets in your area. You can find them in cities, suburbs, and large towns. Also notice all the boutique or artisan tomatoes, melons, eggplants, and squash. You might be able to start your own business growing your own specialty items or buying produce from local farmers and bringing it into the city to sell at farmers' markets.

At the very least, if you have a backyard, consider growing a garden to raise some of your own food. Just out of prison, you will find grocery store vegetables and fruit expensive.

## Lawn Maintenance

A lot of people with expensive homes and busy lives need help around the house. They might hire you to mow the lawn, and then ask if you can paint the garage, or clean their gutters.

Just look for elderly homeowners, single parents, or professional couples who are too old or busy to do their own yard work and have the income to hire somebody. The work can consist of weeding, mulching, cutting grass, trimming hedges, or planting flowers. In the fall you might rake leaves, and in the winter clear sidewalks and driveways of snow and ice.

We suggest you walk the neighborhood, look for yards that need attention, and knock on doors to ask if people need help. The homeowners may even have the tools and machines you need in their garage or shed. Just charge a little less than the competition, and be careful to take good care of their equipment.

After you have a few customers, you might want to make up a business card or flyer promoting your services along with your contact information. Post your flyer on bulletin boards at local businesses around town.

Once you get your business going, you might have the cash to purchase the tools and implements you need at garage sales or through online sites like www.craigslist.com. Eventually, you will buy some tools like a wheelbarrow, trimmer, and other professional-style power implements. As your business gets bigger, you might buy a pickup truck and a trailer to haul your lawn tractor and snow blower. Ideally, you will build a business that follows the four seasons so that you always have a way to pay your bills.

## Arts and Craft Shows

If you are the artistic type, take some time to browse through summer art fairs. You will notice there are many types of artwork and crafts for sale. Talk to the vendors and take some notes as to what products sell well. For example, you might notice the jewelers selling inexpensive earrings and rings that do quite well, while those displaying high-priced pieces made from gold and silver have few customers. Also, check out the people selling birdhouses, yard ornaments, and relatively small and inexpensive paintings. Walk the fair and research what you might be interested in producing yourself.

Many artists spend most of the year at home in their studio or workshop. Then they apply for entry to summer art fairs where they sell their wares. Some of them make a very handsome income. Many of these are family businesses that travel from state to state doing many art fairs in a year.

## Home Repair and Maintenance

You might consider starting a home repair and maintenance business. This could include interior and exterior painting, and drywall, plaster, ceramic tile, and wood floor installation. Over time you could develop the skills to do entire remodeling projects.

The most important thing about home improvement is to be honest about what you can and cannot do. Be careful not to get in over your head. While you might be able to install an outlet or light fixture, leave the serious electrical or plumbing repairs to a licensed contractor, and don't touch the HVAC systems.

You can slowly build a neighborhood business doing home repair, remodeling, and maintenance. You can become the honest, friendly jack-of-all-trades. Over time you can buy tools, a van with your name on the side, distribute business cards, advertise in the Yellow Pages, and become a pillar of the community. Maybe you can even take some courses at the technical schools to upgrade your skills or get licensed in one or more of the builder trades. We can promise you one thing, if you are a good at home repair you will never be out of work.

## Home Daycare

Many mothers earn extra cash by taking in children. As a convicted felon, however, you may find it difficult to be officially licensed for home childcare. Nevertheless, you might still earn a few bucks every week looking after your neighbor's children.

## Home Beauty Care

Women in particular might consider doing home beauty care. This might include cutting or braiding hair and providing manicures, pedicures, and facials. You might also take a few courses at the local technical school. Explore the law governing licenses in your state, and if you are able to get a license, consider starting your own legal salon business or go to work for an existing shop.

## Home Cleaning Service

Many families hire people to come into their homes and do a regular and thorough housecleaning. Once they hire somebody, like their work, and are comfortable with them in their home, they might employ this person for many years.

Of course, as an ex-convict the problem might be your criminal background. Both homeowners and businesses are concerned about cleaning staff who might be tempted to steal. There are ways around this. First, wherever you work, just tell them the truth. This is better that having them find out when they run a criminal background check.

Second, if you are working informally under the table, off the books, tell your clients the truth. Just make sure you don't clean a home for some dishonest rich folk who report their family jewels missing to collect the insurance money, and then try to blame the phony theft on you!

Most families will consider employing you if you are honest with them. They will probably be more concerned about the quality of your work and what you charge per hour than your past.

Some businesses hire ex-convicts because they have applied to state or federal programs that provide employment bonding services. Insurance companies sell bonding policies that insure a company against being sued for employee damage to property, theft, and/ or robbery. As many private insurance companies do not want to bond people with criminal records, the government has special programs that do. Some of these programs even subsidize the wages paid to ex-convicts.

Finally, one of the best ways around the criminal background check problem is the following: if you own the cleaning company, which means you hire and fire workers, but you don't actually do the cleaning or maintenance work, then you don't need to be bonded.

## Internet Businesses

The advent of e-commerce and auction sites like www.ebay.com and www.craigslist.org has certainly facilitated the rise in Internet business. You might begin by selling your unwanted or unused goods on eBay or craigslist. One of the benefits of eBay is that your earnings are clearly posted online. If you have to explain to your PO how you earned enough money to pay for your new Harley, the evidence is there. The only predictable hassle will be the actual work of going to wholesalers, thrift stores, or yard sales to purchase items at rock-bottom prices, monitoring your website or account, securely wrapping the goods to sell, and then carrying it to the local post office. Be careful not to strain your back.

### Freelance Writing or Editing

If you are a skilled writer or editor, you might be able to secure part-time gigs as a freelancer. You could post your expertise on a website or on fliers near community colleges or universities.

If it is not too demeaning, you might make a living typing papers for college students. While we can't guarantee that you will be the next successful ex-convict author like Jack London, Don Pearce, or Edward Bunker, it sure beats living on the streets.

### Providing Services or Programs for Formerly Incarcerated People

After years in prison and on parole, you should know a lot about community services and programs for ex-convicts and parolees. Once you have completed all of your sentence and are discharged from custody, you might think about working in "corrections." There are many nonprofit agencies and companies that operate services for prisoners in the community. Some of them actually hire former prisoners. For example, check out Volunteers of America, Dismas House, Salvation Army, St. Vincent de Paul, and Goodwill.

There are even a few Departments of Corrections that hire ex-convicts as social workers, teachers, nurses, or chaplains. Both private- and public-sector corrections agencies and institutions are especially interested in hiring ex-convicts with college degrees.

Your experience in jail or prison gives you unique insight into the needs of people who journey through the criminal justice system. Having been through the process yourself, you know where people fall through the cracks. Depending upon your education, experience, and business skills, you might consider learning about these businesses that specifically serve this growing population.

We have met some ex-convicts who operate successful halfway houses, job training programs, and alcohol and drug treatment programs. You must first gain some experience working in one of these programs. As an ex-convict you will see services that are not provided, individuals who are underserved, and clients who are not served well. Eventually, you might develop your own innovative idea for a program or service that will help people.

Whatever business you are thinking about starting, take your time setting your plans in motion. Initially, you might want to work for somebody else to learn the ropes. Once you have a good grasp of the business, write up a business plan and run it by your family, your banker, or financial adviser for their input.

## Do You Really Want to Buy a Car?

One of your goals of working might be to buy a car, which will make it easier to get to work. However, if you do not need to, don't drive. We know you want to buy a car. The problem is, the most common way police make arrests is through traffic stops. Once you get behind the wheel, you are subject to searches without a warrant, sobriety tests, and general harassment.

If you must buy a car, try to register it in someone else's name, for example your wife, girlfriend, mother, or brother. Make sure they have no criminal record, a relatively clean driving record, and no outstanding warrants, driving citations, or parking tickets. In most states you will need at least liability insurance. Make sure you keep the auto registration and auto insurance cards in the glove box. Keep the car title at your house; you don't want somebody to steal the car and find the title.

We also suggest you think about what types of cars draw heat. Besides purple Cadillacs with Vouge tires and BMWs with Grateful Dead bumper stickers, we suggest you avoid driving any car more than 10 years old, unless it is a mini van with a PTA sticker. At the very least, check all your lights, fix the loud muffler, and keep the heap clean. If you have to drive an old car, pick something modest and respectable-looking, like a family sedan or van.

If you like pick-up trucks, get rid of the gun rack, check the back for open beer cans, and never carry a weapon (or what might be construed as a weapon) of any kind in the cab, including hunting knives, screwdrivers, baseball bats, or tire irons. Whatever you buy or drive, search the car looking for dope or drug paraphernalia. Yes, we have heard of people buying used cars and then finding plastic bags and joints under the seats. Obviously, it is better if you find these items before the police search your car.

As an ex-convict, you do not want the license plates in your name. The police will "run your tags," discover that you are a parolee, pull over the vehicle, call for backup, and order you out of the car, maybe even pointing a gun at your head. They will order you to the pavement, and maybe even use a shotgun to help you spread your legs. The next thing you know, six or more of the city's finest are standing over you with guns drawn, batons ready, taser weapons charging.

We suggest you protect yourself by letting someone else drive, when at all possible. This is especially true at night, after the bars close, and in high-crime neighborhoods. Just sit in the back and pretend you have a chauffeur.

# Chapter 12

## Special Problems for Jill Convict

Although men and women face many of the same problems when leaving jail or prison, female ex-convicts must deal with a number of special circumstances. This is especially true if they are mothers whose children have been taken away from them by social services, and/or they are in the custody of their relatives and/or abusive and passive-aggressive husband.

Criminologists suggest that females commit different crimes than men. Technically, this is not entirely true. Men and women do the same crimes, but in different proportions. Women are best known for embezzlement, employee theft, passing bad checks, credit card fraud, shoplifting, and prostitution. Women are not commonly convicted of rape, bank robbery, or strong-arm robbery. Traditionally, it was thought that women were less likely than men to be convicted of violent crime outside the immediate family.

Unfortunately, as more women work outside the home, more of them are convicted of the same crimes as men. Many females found they could support themselves selling drugs, fencing hot goods, or managing assorted rackets or scams.

Some illegal enterprises may offer women more equal opportunity than legal occupations. For example, we have heard of women who have worked for the Colombian Drug Cartel. They spoke a number of languages, had college degrees, and managed long-distance operations marketing marijuana and cocaine deliveries all over the world. Like their male counterparts, they were sophisticated business people. Despite gender stereotypes, these females served as directors of large illegal corporations that generated huge profits.

Nevertheless, most women drug dealers are, like the men, small time. They sling dope as a means to buy diapers and food, pay the rent and utilities, and buy clothes for their children. They might well prefer a reasonably well-paid job in a factory or office. The problem is, all they can get is a minimum-wage job that won't cover their household bills. So they sell drugs and take their chances with the police.

Some women grow up in difficult circumstances where they are forced to go to work on the street at an early age. There are 15- and 16-year-old girls in adult state prisons. A lot of female prisoners have been locked up since they were juveniles. They may have been incarcerated because they ran away from home, hung out with the wrong crowd, or were considered incorrigible or uncontrollable.

While in prison they miss the homecoming dance, the senior prom, and an opportunity to date and learn about appropriate relationships with men. They grow up in prison wearing a convict uniform, usually a jumpsuit or industrial uniform. They never get a chance to shop for their own clothes. Nobody shows them pretty dresses, how to pull on tights, or walk in heels. There is no opportunity to learn about make-up, hair color, or ways to curl or straighten their hair. In prison they have no choice but to dress, talk, and walk more like men than women. When they get out of prison, it should be their choice to decide how they dress and live in a gendered society. This is not easy to do all at once.

## Being a Mother Behind Bars

By some estimates, one third of the female population entering jail or prison is pregnant. This should not be so surprising, considering that most women convicts are young adults of childbearing age. They enter prison and hope for the best.

Jails or prison are not the best places to be an expectant mother. Despite the numbers of pregnant prisoners, most correctional institutions are not prepared for the large numbers they now have. There may be little attention paid to prenatal care. Correctional facilities are not known for high-quality medical services. Typically, expectant women will see a nurse but not a doctor in prison. They eat the same prison food as everybody else. Correction institutions are not known for their high-quality food.

In many correctional systems, when a woman goes into labor she is transported to a nearby hospital. This is because the prison wants her to get good medical care. They also want to avoid lawsuits. The problem is, it can take a long time to walk a pregnant prisoner from a cellblock through security at the front gate to the ambulance. Some women's correctional facilities use pickup trucks or golf-cart-type electric vehicles to speed up the process.

The time of delivery is complicated by the fact that some expectant mothers have false labors. This is when the mom has irregular contractions occurring at unpredictable intervals, which may feel the same as real labor. Given all the uncertainty with predicting when true labor begins, some women give birth in prison cells or in the back of ambulances on the way to the hospital.

There are so many expectant mothers in large jails in big cities, and in large federal and state prisons, that some of them have their own obstetricians and maternity wards on-site. This may save the trip to the hospital. Still, Rikers Island (New York City) or Cook County Jail (Chicago) is not exactly what you would like to see on your child's birth certificate. Besides, you better hope the birth is easy, as this is not the Mayo Clinic.

Although the women prefer to give birth in an outside hospital, this too, is not without concerns. Typically, prison guards escort the mother-to-be to the hospital. As prisoners they are required to wear handcuffs and leg irons. For obvious reasons, the officers usually forgo requiring the mother to wear the belly chain, which is usually connected to the handcuffs.

However, many states still require female convicts to wear restraints at the hospital, even while in labor and giving birth. The woman is handcuffed to the bed during labor, while delivering, and after. The connets tell us that doctors are known to argue with the guards, insisting that the restraints be removed. Apparently the prison is concerned that the new mother might give birth, desert the baby, and escape to some far-off land.

In some respects, prison is just like the free world, where some people die and others are born. Once the infant is born, it may be the saddest time for the mother. After carrying the child for nine months, the mother is separated from the child. The social worker must decide on the most appropriate placement of the baby.

Ideally, the father or immediate family of the father or mother might step forward to take the child home. If this is not possible, the newborn might spend a few days at the hospital and then go to an orphanage or foster home. Beyond talking to the father and families, the mother has very little to say about what happens to her child.

The mother is not allowed to bond with the baby. She might spend a day or two in the hospital, depending upon her medical condition. Once the doctor in charge releases her, she is immediately returned to prison. She goes home to an 8-by-10-foot cell or crowded dormitory, where she lies in bed and cries.

Back at the prison, the connets tend to her emotional health. They know that bringing a newborn into this world only to have it ripped from your embrace is tough. It is one of those events you never forgive or forget. A few days later, mom is back on her feet pacing the hallways, staring out the window, her heart filled with grief. A month or two later it will be like the birth never happened. In prison, the outside world fades into the distance.

When mothers get out of the joint, they must attend to children who have been raised by other people, with relatives, in foster homes, or institutions. After mommy has been behind bars for 5 or 10 years, her child may not even recognize her. In some cases, the children may not even want to be returned to their biological mother. Some kids might even prefer orphanages and foster homes, and refuse to go home with their mothers.

Whatever the situation may be, when a mother leaves prison, she goes looking for her children. We have talked to women prisoners who only know their child or children from photographs. One mom had twins in prison. She then completed five years behind bars before she saw them again. The children were too young to understand that they were born in prison and that their mother had just gotten out.

We offer one piece of advice to female prisoners who gave birth in prison: tell your children the truth. They need to know how their life started, and who their biological parents are. This is better than concealing the truth and beginning their lives with a lie.

## Mothers Coming Out of Jail or Prison

Parents, regardless of gender, have some of the same concerns. While men are less likely to return home as custodial parents, women expect to assume this role even if they are a single parent. In some cases, they may be just days or weeks out of prison when they are forced to accept responsibility for their children. While this is something she may eventually want, the connet may be unprepared for the task. This is especially true if she has no place to live, and no job to pay the rent. This can put a great deal of stress upon these women.

Typically, a female parolee mother will go home to live with her own mother. Given that she has no money, job, or place to live on her own, she has little choice. She will stay with her mother until she gets back on her feet.

### Jill Goes Home

You may recall that the DOC dropped Jill off at her parents' home where she will live with her children until she gets back on her feet.

Her parents live in a modest brick bungalow with three bedrooms and one bath. There are two bedrooms on the first floor and one on the second. Jill and the children take over the second floor. The house is old, but well cared for as her dad is good at home repairs.

Her father is a retired factory worker, mom was always a home-maker, and they live on Social Security and a small pension. The home is small but cozy. Her parents are happy to have her home. Despite some initial bumps along the road, the kids lived with their grandparents while Jill was behind bars.

The first few weeks after Jill's release go relatively well. During the day the children are at school, while Jill goes out to look for work. When the school day ends, Jill picks the children up with her father's car. She has a few job prospects. They may pan out. But she is in no rush because at least she has a roof over her and the children's heads.

In the evenings they cook together as Jill tries to supervise her kids' homework. Eventually, she realizes that she is the odd woman out. She upsets the apple cart. There are going to be some arguments. She wants to reassert her authority over the children but feels like her parents get in the way.

Her parents love her, but they are also tired of taking care of her kids and they want a little peace and quiet. Lord knows they deserve it. Eventually, Jill feels like it is time to leave and move on.

This arrangement was only till she got on her feet. Hopefully, the stay is relatively pleasant and she can take some time before finding a place of her own. Eventually, she will pack up her chil-dren and their belongings and move out.

Jill still does not have a job or the money to pay for an apartment. Her only immediate option might be moving to a family shelter. This, however, is moving back to the twilight zone.

We know of some urban shelters for women that have social work-ers and volunteers who help prepare women for employment. They provide temporary housing at the shelter or nearby hotels while the women look for work. But the stay is limited.

Another option might be that Jill moves out of her parents' house when she reconnects with her husband or boyfriend, or starts liv-ing with a girlfriend she met in the joint. Wherever she lives, and with whom, she will have to inform her parole officer (PO) of the change of address.

The PO may need to approve of her living arrangements. He or she may even run criminal background checks on her family or friend. More than likely the PO will make a home visit. This may be scheduled or unannounced.

## The First Few Weeks

The first few weeks may be the toughest. Jill will go from the slow, monotonous speed of prison to the much faster pace of the free world. Her ability to reorganize herself may be determined in part by the experiences she had behind bars, and how psychologically and emotionally ready she is to take on the challenges of life on the outside. She will have to gather all the courage she has to make a new start.

Women are often totally overwhelmed when they return home. As bad as prison was, she only had to take care of herself. Life on the outside is more complicated. In many cases, women prisoners go home to a mess, a family in disarray, and folks with all kinds of problems that will demand her attention. The transition from sole survivor to taking care of everyone else is difficult.

Traditionally, women are expected to be caretakers, the person who raises the children and cares for the sick and elderly. If this role is immediately thrust upon her, it may mean that the ex-convict will be doing a lot of chores she didn't have to do in prison. These include cooking meals, changing diapers, watching children, doing laundry, making beds, and cleaning house.

Jill's outside quality of life will also in part be determined by the dependents who wait for her return. Every family is a different combination of grandparents, parents, children, and grandchildren. She will need to sort out social, emotional, and financial issues. The social calculus of how her family has functioned over time can be difficult to compute. There is so much time to make up and so many needs unmet. She may have no idea where to start.

We suggest that you slowly do a social inventory of your dependents. Take out a pad of paper. At the top of each page write the name of each person in your immediate family. Begin with yourself, then children, parents, and siblings. Below each name write information like age, school, job, health, and medical status. Then add notes relevant to each person. Pay careful attention to physical, social, and emotional needs. Use the note pad to get a handle on what changes have occurred while you were away. Then try to determine your responsibilities and daily duties. Do not forget to include yourself on your list.

## Which Jill Convict Is Returning Home?

Out of prison and out of her mother's house, Jill must finally confront who she is. She is in a precarious situation. Jill has played the role of the good convict and the loyal daughter, but now she must confront her own identity. This can run the gambit from her work identity to her sexual orientation.

Years in prison can change a person. Some of the changes are unintentional. Maybe others just come with the territory where modifications are predictable. Others are a surprise. Then one day the gate opens and you step out into the free world. Inside it was a single-gender world. Outside there are two genders.

What if Jill had drifted into a lesbian sexual orientation while in prison? While her sexual preference was heterosexual on the street, in prison homosexuality was her only choice if she required affection. So which Jill is returning home? Does she even know?

## Entering the Twilight Zone

After a few months of living with her parents, Jill found herself and the children living in the twilight zone. With no money, she was forced to take the children to a temporary shelter.

Beyond the bars of prison there is a dimly lit world of temporary shelters, halfway houses, and cheap motels. Jill is no longer in the dark of prison, but neither is she in the light of freedom. The first few weeks out of a correctional facility, many women bounce around from one living arrangement to another. Transitional or temporary housing arrangements only add to their disorientation.

Jill enters a world beyond prison but still on the margins of respectable society. At the halfway houses she meets people like herself coming out of prison. She also meets people on their way in. At least once a week, the police and POs come and take people away. Other folks are in and out of hospitals or mental health facilities.

A lot of these people are in worse shape than the men and women coming out of correctional facilities. Some of them live on the streets for years. They come to the shelters for food, showers, and some respite from the cold. These are the homeless vagabonds who live in the shadows of the city. Many of them are former prisoners and will be again. The only freedom they know is squatting in abandoned buildings or sleeping under bridges.

Jill brings her young children to the shelter. What does she do with them when she goes out to look for a job? Who will look after them? Will her kids feel safe in the presence of so many strangers?

Jill hopes there will be an on-site daycare or an affordable daycare center nearby where she can drop the children off for a couple of hours. Jill also hopes she can find a shelter where they will have individual rooms for families so they don't have to sleep in the dormitory.

For Jill, her children may help her to stay straight, to stabilize and find her way in the dim light of the twilight zone. They may prevent her from drinking, using drugs, and sleeping with strange men. They reinforce her primary role as a mother. The kids also remind her of what she could be if she gets back on her feet.

Jill sees men and women at the beginning and the end of their trek through the perpetual incarceration machine. The shelters are just one stop along the way for convicts who become homeless, and the homeless who go in and out of jail.

Their trans-incarceration may last for many years and take them through multiple roles as sick, mad, or dangerous. Jill wonders how she compares, what she might look like to others, and how far down the road to recovery or oblivion she has gone. Sometimes a person gets lost along the way.

Fortunately, Jill spends only a few weeks at the community shelter. In her monthly meeting with her PO, she tells him that she is not especially comfortable there. The PO suggests that she should go to the Salvation Army where they have better accommodations for families.

Jill hopes she likes the Salvation Army better. She needs to save some money so she can get a place of her own. Jill packs up her stuff in plastic garbage bags and goes to the Salvation Army.

## Sharing a Small Apartment

Jill takes her children to the Harbor Light Center managed by the Salvation Army. This community-based rehabilitation center is an old brick apartment building that was renovated some 30 years ago and is now showing its age. Here Jill lives with two other women in a two-bedroom apartment. Each bedroom has bunk beds for two of the residents. Jill gets her own bedroom, sharing the bunk bed with the kids.

Jill and her children eat some of their meals at the nearby soup kitchen. The standing in line and talking to people reminds her of prison, except in this line there are men, women, and children. Other days she prepares meals at the apartment with food she receives at the food bank. She also works a few hours a day at the thrift store, where she is able to find some clothes to wear on job interviews.

The people at the Salvation Army are very kind. They don't mind that she was unable to pay her weekly charge for room and board. They never bring it up or say a word. Instead, they assign her a social worker and try to help her apply for jobs. On some days she dresses up and goes out to search for work. She fills out applications, but nobody calls to offer her an interview. Instead she continues to work at the thrift store, and although she's technically considered a volunteer, they give her a few dollars each day so she has money for bus tickets, smokes, and coffee.

The officers and soldiers of the Salvation Army are devoted to their clients. They never ask her about her criminal record; it doesn't matter to them. Although they have a service contract with the state DOC, they have no interest in administering alcohol or drug tests. Jill is happy she was not tested. She can come as she pleases, and feels safe from being violated and returned to prison. Jill appreciates the trust and confidence the Salvation Army has in her. She spends six months at the Salvation Army.

## Social Judgments Beyond Jill's Control

Women may be more sensitive than men about what other people think about them. However, their feelings may be a detriment to beginning a new life. We suggest that Jill remember that better days are on the way.

Jill Convict has no control over the social judgments of others. Age, appearance, and race especially affect women. Being young and attractive may help her get a job. Then again, it might attract the wrong kind of men. Being a little older may help her to maintain her dignity. Although we might wish people were color-blind, race is still a factor where one lives and works. The point is that every Jill is different.

## Shame Leads to Isolation

Women tend to feel more shame for their crimes than men do. Society may have stricter standards for women than men. For example, women may be more ashamed of their dependency on alcohol or drugs. They may try to hide their addiction. This shame can lead to social isolation because other people don't accept the lies and the deceit.

What is the point of pretending to be somebody that you're not? How can you make new friends if you present a false front? We suggest that Jill tell the truth when making new friends, no matter how difficult. Telling the truth is much simpler than trying to fool people. The truth enables other people to understand, offer assistance, and accept you as a real person.

Once you have found the courage to be yourself, people will want to be your friend. We suggest that you learn to be selective with friends. You don't need to be popular or surround yourself with a new crew, posse, or collection of cool people. Just try to get to know people one at a time, and make friends slowly.

A good friend is one who tells you the truth, is there for you in good times and bad, and shares a piece of your life. A good friend won't care that you were in prison. She will be the person who has known you many years and knows you as a person. Just remember not to become too dependent on your friends, as they have their own lives to live.

## Dependency

Some women become prisoners in disguise. They hook up with a man and depend on him for everything. They become homemakers without an education, vocation, or profession. The man pays all the bills, makes most of the decisions, and has most of the power in the relationship. What if he loses his job, leaves you for another woman, or suddenly passes away?

Dependency implies a loss of freedom. We want Jill to be a self-supporting person. Ideally, she should not rely entirely on anybody for the basic necessities of life. This means she should complete enough formal education to compete for well-paying jobs. She should work at least part-time outside the home.

We suggest that Jill build vocational or career options for herself so she can work and pay her own way if necessary. This gives her a work record and helps build up her resumé. It also gives her some say in how income is spent, bills are paid, and savings are planned.

Jill needs to understand that freedom is more than staying out of jail or prison. She also needs freedom to grow and be herself. While we all sacrifice some liberties to build a relationship and there is always a degree of dependency, this does not mean we have to be totally dependent. Our advice is that Jill needs to build reciprocal relationships where people have both rights and responsibilities that are open for discussion and negotiation.

## Sexual Assault

There is a lot of research suggesting that many connets have been the victims of sexual assault sometime in their life. They may have been raped by a family member, acquaintance, stranger, or even correctional officer in jail or prison. We know that these assaults may figure prominently as triggers for alcohol or drug abuse, or other crimes.

We have heard the story of a woman who for 20 years was a high school teacher in a small town in the Midwest. Most of her adult life she repressed the memory of being raped as a young girl. Years later, after she had graduated from college and established herself in her chosen profession, the memory returned. As she was too busy, or maybe ashamed, to seek counseling, she took comfort in prescription drugs and booze. Over time she drank more and more, first at home and then at the bars. One night she drove her car into a tree.

Seriously injured in the car crash, she was also arrested for drunk driving. After her conviction, she was fired from her position at a small-town high school. Unable to secure another job teaching, she took a minimum-wage job at a supermarket. The loss of income contributed to her divorce and eventually the loss of her home.

She returned to the bars, became a regular customer, and then was busted for another DUI. This time she got jail time and probation. The former schoolteacher was violated on probation and sent to prison to finish her sentence.

Most POs would say her problem was booze. We contend that a more careful reading of her story would suggest that the repressed memory of the sexual assault precipitated a downward spiral that led to the drinking, which eventually resulted in the teacher becoming a convict.

The real question is: why did she never receive help for the original problem? She never told the police, judge, or PO about the rape. Because of her feeling of shame or the belief that she needed to remain silent about the event, she never told criminal justice personnel. Thus, there was no recommendation for therapy.

Even if she had discussed the sexual assault with them, there may have been no funding to pay for the therapist. Her inability to face the truth about her horrific experience as a young girl contributed to her slide from respectable schoolteacher to convict in prison.

The repressed truth haunted her life, contributed to her drinking, and brought her down. She was victimized twice by the same assault. While we applaud her for trying to tough it out on her own, the moral of our story is that women need to demand help. They need to consult with qualified professionals who can help them uncover repressed experiences, learn to live with them, and find relief from subconscious memories that hurt.

Typically women's prisons have staff with undergraduate degrees in social work or social science, but they usually don't have psychiatrists or psychologists on staff. Volunteers from the outside operate groups that can be effective in helping women deal with the painful experiences in their lives. However, prison is never a great place to deal in depth with these intimate memories and feelings.

There are many different Jills walking out of prison. Each one has her own complex life history. Somehow, they have to come to terms with who they were and find the strength to become who they want to be despite the rough road they travel.

# Epilogue

## Freedom as a Felon in the United States

After getting out of prison, both Joe and Jill have different fates.

Joe eventually found a stable job working first as a carpenters' apprentice, and now as a journeyman. After a couple of bumps along the road, he got his union ticket and is now a well-respected shop steward in his local union.

His prison experience taught him how to negotiate. This comes in handy dealing with the numerous conflicts he encounters between his co-workers and job foremen. The good news is that a large subdivision is being built in a nearby suburb where he lives. He should have plenty of work for a couple years.

Joe is now married with two children. He and his wife are saving money to build their dream home. In many respects, Joe caught a lucky break.

Jill found a job as a cook trainee in a fancy restaurant. Unfortunately, a jealous co-worker thought she was getting preferential treatment. The co-worker made up a story about Jill stealing liquor and reported her to management. Shortly after this incident, the boss let her go.

Jill burned through her meager savings in no time. Without a job, she couldn't make it out of the shelter and rent a place of her own. This forced her to send her children back to her folks. Desperate for cash, she started slinging dope, was arrested shortly thereafter, and is now doing another stretch in state prison. Life's not fair, especially for men and women out on parole.

We wrote this book to help you get a better handle on life beyond bars. The advice we offer is based not only on scholarly research but on what we have learned from both personal experience and talking with prisoners, ex-convicts, correctional staff, and probation and parole officers (PO). We hope your reading helps you to better understand the complex problems formerly incarcerated people encounter in our society.

In this chapter we close with some thoughts that some readers may find controversial. Only dangerous human beings belong locked in cages. There are hundreds of thousands of relatively harmless people in prison, and we believe they don't belong there.

## Freedom in a Strange Land?

In the United States we value freedom above else. Beginning in the seventeenth century, pilgrims, serfs, and farmers left their homes in distant lands to build new lives in America. They wanted freedom from religious persecution, debtor prisons, forced conscription, and grinding poverty. They crossed the oceans in wooden ships to worship as they please and for an opportunity to work their own land.

Some people paid for their passage as indentured servants. Others came as prisoners or slaves locked in cages or chained to the floor below the decks of ships. Many of the immigrants dreamed of a better life. The convicts and slaves just hoped to survive the passage and the bondage to come.

In some respects, we might think of modern-day convicts also as immigrants to a strange land. They journey on a forced passage they did not choose. After years behind bars, they hoped for a better life beyond bars. Despite the mistakes they made that sent them to prison, they do not take their freedom for granted. Nearly every man and woman getting out of a correctional institution wants to do good, to make a new start. Trust us: nobody wants to go back to prison.

By now you realize that the labels "felon" and "ex-convict" mark a person for life. Most people avoid or exclude from their lives individuals who have just gotten out of jail or prison. You can hear them whispering behind your back or making polite excuses why they can't (or don't want to) help you.

Despite felony convictions and prison records, this is America, the land of second chances. No matter who you are or where you have been, once you have completed your criminal sentence you have the right to be free again. So hold your head up, and don't accept the stigma that people and organizations may force on you. Let them know you paid for your transgressions.

## Walking Down Paper

Prison is no cakewalk, and neither is the post-prison experience. At each stage of the perpetual incarceration machine, you will face different challenges. Surviving prison and parole require patience and humility. In many respects the struggle is more mental than physical. The real threat is to your sanity. Take the pain, do not give in to fear, and fight to maintain your dignity. As the months and years pass, it gets easier.

Getting out of prison is no picnic, either. Prisoners call parole "doing paper" or "on paper." They talk about "walking down paper" as completing years on parole. The first year or two, a person is ordered to report to the parole office anywhere from once a week to once a month. As time goes by, and it appears as if you are con-forming to the rules and regulations, the parole office may cut you some slack. Then the PO may decide to require report dates once every three months, and then once every six months. Eventually you become a "paper man." You just mail in monthly reports list-ing where you live, work, and what you earn. Your PO may do a home visit—scheduled or unannounced—once a year. In some states, your PO may even decide to reward you for good behavior by applying for your early release from parole.

Most of this book has focused on the first few months of freedom from prison. Many people manage to be free for at least six months. About half the people coming out of prison will go back before they complete parole or community supervision. Their PO sees that they can't hold a job or establish a residence. Failing to make progress, struggling on the street, their homeless life is cold and lonely, barely better than what they had in prison.

Sooner or later they screw up, fail a drug test, or get arrested for a misdemeanor, and get violated. Sometimes the PO just decides to yank on their leash before they catch a more serious case. He sends them back to prison for their own good, before they really screw up.

The other half will successfully walk down paper, receive a certificate or letter of completion, and finally be free. They will no longer be in custody. But they are not as free as most Americans. Although you are a now an *ex-convict*, you will never be an *ex*-felon unless you miraculously get your conviction overturned or pardoned.

Instead, you will be a felon for life, subject to the same federal restrictions and different state sanctions, depending upon where you were convicted and where you reside. Wherever you live, your past felony conviction may attract police attention.

If you are arrested, your felony status will affect how you are treated. If you are charged or indicted again, your past record will make it harder for you to defend yourself. Convicted again, you will receive a harsher sentence. In most states, you may even get a life sentence under habitual criminal or three-strikes legislation.

Frequently we hear sad stories like this. A teenager is convicted of rape and murder. He serves 20 years in a maximum-security penitentiary for his crime. After completing 18 years behind bars, he is then released to serve the remainder of his life on parole.

The man becomes a model citizen, goes to work every day, gets married, buys a home, and becomes a parent. He reports to the parole office every month for many years, until he becomes a "paper man."

As the years pass, he forgets about prison and parole. He never talks about it with his wife or children. Meanwhile, the political climate in his state is changing. The legislature wants tougher laws, more law and order. A newspaper digs up old stories about violent crimes. A two-minute story about his crime appears on the local newscast. His PO decides to visit his home and search the premises. He finds a firearm or recreational drugs.

Then, despite the fact that the parolee has been a law-abiding citizen for many years, he is returned to prison.

The bottom line is, most people have no idea what you have been through, and probably don't care. They don't know you have actually paid for your crimes.

## Too Many Wars

Clearly, many factors have affected the increase in the number of people sent to prison and thus getting out. But one of the biggest problems for both state and federal correctional systems is the back end of the process. There are not enough resources available for those people getting out of jail and prison.

We are not just talking about parole offices and POs, or money for their laptops and tracking devices. We need to provide private agencies with more funding so that they can deliver meaningful support and post-prison-rehabilitative services for their clients.

### The War on Drugs

The United States is waging wars on multiple fronts. There are the foreign wars like in Iraq and Afghanistan. Then there are the domestic battles the government is fighting at home against people who drink and drive, use or sell recreational drugs, or join urban gangs.

The war on drugs was started by President Nixon in 1970, intensified by President Reagan in 1980, and continues today unabated. After nearly 40 years, and millions of arrests, there is no end.

We all would like to reduce drunken driving, drug abuse, and gang activity. But there are no simple solutions and easy fixes. What we do know is that a warlike approach to these social problems creates more victims than heroes. The military approach should end now, peace be declared, and a new positive direction taken.

We need to recognize that most alcohol and drug abusers are not dangerous criminals. They have a problem we can solve with medical attention, community care, residential alcohol and drug treatment, and employment counseling and job training. Most people who join gangs do so out of a need to belong or the lack of meaningful opportunities.

You might live in a neighborhood with dope dealers working street corners, drug addicts entering in and out of crack houses, and gang-style drive-by shootings. So you want the police to do something about it. We wish the answer was simply arresting lawbreakers and sending them to jail or prison. Unfortunately, there are always replacements—corner boys or wannabes—willing to take the place of those imprisoned.

There are no easy answers for crime reduction. However, we do know that the new direction should include more resources for fragile families, better public schools, and employment opportunities. We can help stabilize families with subsidized childcare, pre-school, and after-school alternatives. In turn, parents need to spend more time with their children and make sure that they go to school and do well in their studies. Parents must also act as law-abiding, responsible role models.

A lot of crime is really "illegal work." We need to address the real rate of unemployment in minority communities. Our country should find a way to put these people back to work. This might include rebuilding urban infrastructure, repairing roads and bridges, and constructing mass transit across America. When we lower the rate of unemployment, reduce poverty, and raise the standard of living, we will reduce both drug-related crime and alcohol dependency.

## The War on Drugs Becomes the War on Terrorism

While the war on drugs continues unabated, by the late 1980s the war on terrorism began. With the passage of the PATRIOT Act (2001), time-honored constitutional guarantees protecting you from unnecessary government intrusion into your life are whittled away.

Government can now look into your financial and personal records. Individuals who consider themselves pacifists and peaceniks are labeled "people of interest," or even worse, put on terrorist watch lists. This process simply opens the door to government fishing expeditions.

In this paranoid national security climate, it is even tougher for people to do well after incarceration. Criminal records, financial records, credit histories, and government intelligence files on association and affiliation are used to sort and segregate suspects. Computer records make it possible to separate the entire U.S. population into separate strata with FICO scores.

Even addresses imply consequences, as finance and insurance companies decide to redline entire neighborhoods as unworthy or high risk. A person's criminal record is public. Anybody willing to pay a nominal fee can go online and check court records. In some states, it is even free. This is now the easiest way to identify or mark individuals as unworthy, untrustworthy, or high security risks.

There are simply too many people in jail and prison. We advocate amnesty for nonviolent drug prisoners after three years or less of incarceration. Jail and prison should serve as a wake-up call to get their attention, dry them out from substance abuse, and start preparing them for a better life. Among the possible solutions is dedicating more resources toward experiments in rehabilitation and restorative justice.

## The One and Only Path: Reforming Rehabilitation

Correctional administrators have nearly given up on rehabilitation, as the majority of their budgets are devoted to salaries and security. Meanwhile, architectural, engineering, and construction companies lobby state legislatures to spend more money on new prisons. Scarce public dollars are squandered on cement, bricks, and steel to build more facilities to house a growing jail and prison population.

Prisons become human warehouses where very little funding is spent on educational and vocational programs. Unfortunately, the performance evaluations of prisons or prison administrators have rarely been tied to rehabilitation, lowering recidivism, or the relative success of prisoners.

Clearly, the lack of meaningful rehabilitation programs in correctional institutions contributes to convicts failing parole and returning to prison. In effect, we have a perpetual incarceration machine that recycles the same people. The prison reproduces its own population of failures, because it does not adequately educate, train, and prepare convicts for life after incarceration. Most convicts and parolees know the score. If they really want to make it, more than likely they will have to do most of the hard work on their own. This usually requires educating themselves about the challenges of reentry.

If we really want to help prisoners, they should be released with Social Security cards, current drivers' licenses, and sufficient gate money for rent and food for at least three months. They should be free of parole and community supervision. We should stop treating them like children, and treat them like adults. This means providing them with the professional services that they request. Let them decide on their own if they need employment assistance, family counseling, drug and alcohol treatment programs, and medical services.

We suggest that probation and parole offices be converted into community resource centers. Retrain the workers to be resource brokers. This redeployment would better serve the needs of ex-convicts and the local community.

Some resource officers might specialize in people coming out of jail or prisons. Others would focus on the homeless, or folks in shelters or living on the street. Looked at with a broader vision, these are the same people at different stages of their journey. These services will help ex-prisoners better adjust to the "free world," thus reducing the likelihood that they will return to a life of crime. In addition, we need smarter ideas to solve the social problems that cause crime. Locking up millions of people in jail and prison is an insult to our collective intelligence. We need to think beyond the bars, reorder our priorities, and, finally, learn to address the root causes of crime and social disorder.

## Restorative Justice

Restorative justice is a movement pioneered by the cultural traditions of the Quakers and Mennonites that calls into question the current practice of criminal justice. It is meant to divert people from jail or prison and promotes their reintegration into the community. The process emphasizes group negotiation, the needs of victims, and the responsibility of defendants to accept the consequences for their behavior. The negotiation usually includes penalties, such as paying restitution and doing community service. The process encourages reconciliation based on repentance, apology, and forgiveness.

It is usually used in juvenile and adult misdemeanor cases where a person pleads guilty. Many court systems call this process a Victim Offender Reconciliation Program (inelegantly dubbed VORP). These VORP Programs are facilitated by trained mediators and employ face-to-face encounters between victim and offender. The mediators usually suggest sanctions that satisfy the court, restore the victim, and reconcile the offender. Even the U.S. Department of Justice has experimented with the idea of restorative justice.

## Converting Prisons Into Residential Treatment Centers (RTC)

The federal government wants to wage a war on drugs, without providing sufficient resources for the victims of drugs. Meanwhile, many communities report a desperate need for publicly funded residential treatment facilities. It can cost $500 or more for one day in a private alcohol or drug treatment center.

Typically, the courts will give probation to middle-class people with adequate private healthcare insurance. The court expects them to complete drug rehabilitation at a private facility or hospital. Some of the poshest locations can charge thousands of dollars a day.

This is well out of the reach of most poor people without healthcare insurance. Even people with insurance don't realize that their policies are inadequate. Sometimes they don't pay enough or the treatment is not of sufficient duration. Folks without insurance must make do with the help they get from free clinics or clergy. Today, most drug offenders without private healthcare insurance go to jail where they must quit cold turkey.

We encourage states to try to handle addictions a new way: through state-run Residential Treatment Centers (RTCs). Each state selects one prison to be converted into an RTC. The prison would decommission the gun towers, turn off the security technology at the perimeter fence, and transfer the entire inmate population to other facilities. Then they would open all security grills, hallway doors and cell house doors, and sally ports (spaces with two locked doors). The prison becomes an open institution.

The DOC then reassigns most of the prison's correctional officers to other facilities. Those with college degrees might apply to be trained to be RTC counselors. Then the prison hires appropriate medical staff, social workers, case managers, counselors, teachers, employment specialists, sociologists, and psychologists. The treatment staff decides how to best use the prison buildings to house and treat the potential patient population.

The state then announces a bold, new initiative based on two simple facts about alcohol and drug addiction. First, the most likely chance for success comes when a person asks for help. The individual has to want to kick the habit. Second, sobriety and freedom from drug addiction take time. People need a few months in residential care where they have no access to chemical substances, and time to detoxify their bodies.

The program invites any citizen in the state to ask for help. He simply goes to an RTC and requests voluntary commitment. The medical staff has him read and sign a basic contract where he asks for three to six months at the RTC. There would be no arrest, conviction, or public record. The state does not charge a penny. The client arrives at the RTC on the scheduled day and stays as specified in the contract.

Think of this as a new approach to crime prevention. For example, an alcoholic who is concerned she might drink and drive again, a husband who behaves violently toward his wife, or a person with a daily cocaine habit might call 911 and ask for help. The 911 operator would direct the individual to the nearest RTC. The idea is to give people the help they need to overcome their difficulties, without sending them off to jail or prison.

A large prison converted to an RTC might serve 2,000 people every 90 days, which means approximately 8,000 people a year. Once the patients arrive at the center, they get a medical exam, social work evaluation, and treatment plan. Depending upon the person, she might complete her GED, get job training, or get counseling while she receives medical attention for her addiction. Relapses or follow-ups could be handled by an outpatient clinic at the RTC.

## How Can We Change Things?

Reforming or changing community corrections starts with questioning our ideas and attitudes about crime, criminals, and correctional facilities. The first step is to change public awareness. People in this country need to know what the prison system in the United States is really like—not how it is presented in movies, television reality shows, or fictional books. Once the public knows it costs $30,000 a year to keep a person in prison, and how ineffective they are at rehabilitation, maybe more people will push for prison reform.

Most Americans have no idea what goes on behind bars and how it affects prisoners, even after they are released. There should be more transparency. Correctional facilities need to be open to inspection and investigation. Prisoners and correctional workers should be allowed to be interviewed more frequently.

We have seen too many reporters and researchers settling for convict and correctional officer interviews that were monitored by the prison administration. Nobody will respond honestly when they know they are being watched by video cameras and the warden's staff. Reporters should also interview prisoners after they get out of correctional facilities, when they have the freedom to describe prison conditions. The public needs to hear the rest of the story.

## America Is the Land of Second Chances

We end this book much as we started, with a plea for second chances. Americans have always pulled for the little guy, the underdog. People coming out of prison are heavily supervised by correctional authorities.

Beyond bars, they are convicts living among us. They are legally semi-citizens. Some felons have to register for life with the police. Others have their photos and criminal records displayed on government websites. In some states they lose the right to vote for life. All felons lose the right to bear arms for life. Most have a very hard time getting back on their feet.

And yet most felons are no different than you or me. They are the men and women who took one too many steps over the line and got caught. Maybe you stepped over the line once or twice, but pulled back before you were arrested. Are you a better person, or just lucky? Maybe one day your fortune will turn and you will need a second chance.

America is the land of nine innings, two halves, and four quarters. No matter the score, there is always another game or season. We were raised to compete, win or lose, and not to be sore losers. This entire book has been about losers asking for a second chance. Every day, men and women all over this country like Joe and Jill Convict walk out of jail or prison. After time behind bars they are sober, clean of drug addiction, eager to work, and desperate to rebuild their lives.

If you give them a chance they may turn out to be your best worker, neighbor, or even spouse. In prison they learned that every society sets limits on our behavior. As they get out of prison they are on their best behavior. It is up to us to give them a second chance.

# Appendix A

## A Glossary of Reentry Terms

Whether you are an ex-convict, a corrections professional, or a volunteer who wants to help people getting out of jail or prison, the following are terms you need to know.

**after care**   Programs and services available in the community for drug addiction, psychological counseling, employment assistance, and medical treatment.

**arraignment**   Defendant's first court appearance, where the criminal charge is read and the defendant enters a plea of guilty or not guilty.

**bail**   Court decides surety necessary to ensure a defendant appears in court. Surety might be cash or property, such as a car, boat, camper or home.

**bail bondsman**   Local business that posts bail in exchange for percent of bond. Usually a bail bond company requires a defendant to pay 10 percent of bail. The defendant does not get this back. The bonding company must guarantee that the defendant appears in court or pay the outstanding bail amount to the court.

**boot camp**   Quasi-military residential prison program for juvenile or young adults.

**citation**   A legal order to appear in court to begin due process procedure connected with possible probation or parole violation.

**civil death**   Term used to describe the loss of certain rights of citizenship by prisoners while they are in prison. Felons may also lose these rights for the rest of their life.

**classification**   A process used in correctional facilities to determine whether a prisoner should be housed in minimum, medium, or maximum security.

**CO**   Correctional Officer.

**cognitive behavioral therapy**   Treatment that helps a person to develop better thinking skills.

**Community Corrections Officer (CCO)**   Department of Corrections employees who work outside prisons, such as at state halfway houses, work-release centers, day centers, or in probation or parole services.

**community service**   Court-imposed sentence or condition of probation that requires offender to work a certain number of hours for local government or a nonprofit agency. This might include picking up litter on highways or in parks, or working at public hospitals or nursing homes.

**concurrent sentence**   Two or more sentences served at the same time.

**conditional release**   The release of a prisoner from jail or prison to community supervision.

**conditions of supervision**   Written rules or mandates concerning behavior of people in community custody. Failure to obey rules may result in arrest, citation, or return to jail or prison.

**consecutive sentences**   Two or more sentences, served one after the other.

**contact visit**   A meeting between an inmate and a visitor in which the two individuals are not separated by glass or screen. May also refer to fact-to-face meeting of parole officer with client.

**continuance**   Postponement of a scheduled court hearing for a good reason.

**contraband**   Anything not authorized to be in possession of person on probation or parole. For example, this could be alcohol, a computer, drugs, or pornography.

**contract**   A written agreement between two or more parties. The contract includes responsibilities of each party, time, process, and resources.

**conviction**   Guilty verdict or a finding of guilt, a plea of guilty, or a plea of *nolo contendere.*

**dance floor**   Prison slang for the prison sitting room.

**day fines**   A fine that takes into consideration not only the severity of the crime but also the daily income of the defendant.

**day reporting center**   Facility in which probationers and parolees are require to report. Some are ordered to participate in substance-abuse counseling, social skills training, or employment training.

**determinate sentencing**   Usually refers to a sentence in which there is no parole. The sentence might be reduced for good time, leaving the convicted individual to serve 85 percent of the sentence before being released.

**dime**   A 10-year sentence.

**diversion program**   Court program in which the defendant gets a chance to avoid jail or prison. Instead, he might get probation or a suspended sentence, and or even avoid having the conviction appear on his record.

**drug and alcohol treatment**   Substance-abuse therapy inside or outside prison; it's usually in the form of group meetings.

**drug courts**   A court designed to divert drug addicts and defendants from jail or prison.

**economic sanctions** Defendant is required to give something of monetary value to the court (such as fines, fee, or property).

**electronic jacket** Computerized criminal history records that are maintained by government.

**electronic monitoring** Surveillance technology used by parole authorities to keep track of people on probation and parole.

**electronic monitoring device** The hardware a probationer or parolee might wear.

**felon** A person convicted of a felony.

**felony** A crime punishable by imprisonment of a year and a day, or more.

**fine** A financial penalty.

**flat time** A prisoner serves her entire sentence without deduction for good time.

**good time** Days subtracted from prison sentence for good behavior.

**habitual offender** A repeat offender, usually given a harsher or longer sentence for second- or third-time offenses.

**halfway houses** Facility managed by federal, state, or contract company where prisoners live.

**house arrest** Court-ordered punishment that requires a prisoner to serve his sentence at home, usually accompanied by electronic monitoring.

**incarceration** Imprisonment.

**indictment** A formal bill or charge usually made by a grand jury.

**intensive supervision** Close tracking of high-risk parolees; the supervision may involve a team of officers and include daily contact, home visits, curfews, and drug tests.

**intermediate punishments**   Also known as intermediate sanctions. They are more severe than probation, but less severe than prison. These might include restitution, community service, day reporting centers, and or electronic monitoring.

**jail**   City or county facility for prisoners awaiting trial, convicted of misdemeanors, or be held before transportation to prison or to another jurisdiction. Most jails are designed to hold inmates for a year or less. In some states prisoners can spend up to five years in jail.

**judicial discretion**   The power that a judge has to decide a legal case, including the type and severity of the sanction.

**mandatory release (MR)**   The release of a convict at the very end or expiration of sentence. The prisoner serves the sentence without deductions for parole release.

**mandatory sentences**   A sentence that must be given by law.

**mediation**   A meeting to work out an agreement or resolve civil or criminal disputes.

**mitigating factors**   Facts or events in the commission of a crime, which may indicate a shorter sentence.

**nickel**   A five-year sentence.

**nolo contendere**   A no-contest plea, with no guilty plea. As there is no guilty plea or confession in the criminal case, it makes it harder for the victim to pursue a civil suit.

**on paper**   Convict slang for serving time on parole.

**paper man**   A parolee who no longer needs to meet with the parole officer. Instead, she just sends in a monthly report.

**parens patriae**   The state assumes the role of parent for a child who is delinquent or abandoned.

**parole**   Period during which a prisoner is let out of jail or prison before the end of his sentence to serve the balance of his sentence out in the community.

**parole board**   Group of individuals who typically meet inside prison to decide whether a prisoner might be released to serve the balance of her remaining sentence in community.

**parole release supervision**   A conditional release granted by the Parole Commission, the court, or the Department of Corrections, allowing a prisoner to serve the remainder of his sentence in the community.

**pee/piss test**   A test in which an individual must pee in a cup and have his urine tested for the presence of drugs or alcohol.

**pre-sentence investigation**   Report prepared by probation or parole officer for the court to be used to determine criminal sentence.

**pre-trial service agency**   Facility to which individuals who have been granted bail or released on their own recognizance must report on a regular basis.

**preliminary hearing**   A hearing in which a court decides if they have the legal authority and cause to hold the defendant in custody for a longer period of time.

**prison**   A state, federal, private, or military facility where a person who is convicted of a crime serves a sentence behind bars. Typically used with individuals who are serving more than a year behind bars.

**probation**   A sentence in which a person convicted of a crime serves her time in the community without being in jail or prison. She may have to comply with court-ordered sanctions.

**pulling a chain**   Convict jargon for serving a sentence.

**pulling a train** Refers to having multiple consecutive sentences. For example, if a convict has two dimes and a quarter, each dime is a boxcar and a quarter is the caboose. He will end up spending a total of 45 years behind bars.

**quarter** A 25-year sentence.

**rap sheet** Informal term for official record of arrests, convictions, and disposition of court cases for an individual.

**recidivism** Usually refers to a parole violation and/or the commission of new crimes that results in a person being returned to jail or prison.

**rehabilitation programs** Programs meant to help people get back on their feet and become productive members of society; it may include vocational or educational programs, job training, or counseling and medical treatment.

**relapse** Usually refers to an alcoholic or drug addict returning to the use or abuse of chemical substances.

**restitution** Court-ordered payments to victim(s).

**restorative justice** Program for community prevention and intervention that brings together the victim and perpetrator to help negotiate a resolution.

**revocation** Administrative or court action that revokes probation or parole for violating the stated conditions, including the commission of a new crime.

**revocation for technical reasons** Administrative or court action that revokes probation or parole for violating the stated conditions—for example, a bad drug test, being in a bar, failing to observe curfew, or failure to report to the parole office—but not the commission of a new crime.

**sentence** The penalty handed down by the judge.

**shock incarceration**   Court sentences first-time minor offender to prison as a means to shock or scare him straight.

**short leash**   Prisoner, probationer, or parolee under close or tight supervision.

**unsupervised probation**   Court-ordered probation with no reporting to the probation/parole office. This is usually reserved for defendants with low risk of violating rules of probation.

**vertical case prosecution**   The same lawyers handle criminal prosecution of cases from beginning to end of the court process.

**victims' services**   Court activities designed to respond to the needs of victims and witnesses.

**walking down paper**   Convict slang for doing time on parole.

# Appendix B

## Organizations That Help Ex-Convicts

There is no reason why you should do this journey alone. There are numerous organizations that help ex-convicts. Some of the more prominent nonprofits are listed in this appendix. They serve ex-convicts, helping them rebuild their lives, find work, and advocate on behalf of re-entry. These groups may provide services both inside prisons and on the outside. Most of these are located in the United States, while some of them have international branches.

### Alcoholics Anonymous

A nondenominational organization established to help recovering or recovered alcoholics. They hold weekly meetings in most communities in the United States and elsewhere. Contact: www.aa.org.

### Convict Criminology Website

The "New School of Convict Criminology" is a relatively new and controversial perspective in the field of corrections and the academic field of criminology. It challenges the way crime and correctional problems are traditionally represented and discussed by researchers, policy makers, and politicians. Contact: www.convictcriminology.org.

### CURE: Citizens United for the Rehabilitation of Errants

Organization that works with prisoners, their families, and interested citizens "to reduce crime through criminal justice reform." They do this through information sharing and contacts with politicians. Started in 1972 in Texas, CURE is organized into state chapters, a federal chapter, and international chapters with headquarters in Washington, D.C. Contact: www.curenational.org.

### Dismas House

This is the name of many halfway houses for people coming out of jail or prison. Many groups all over the country use this name. The original Dismas House was established in 1974 as part of the Vanderbilt prison project. Another successful one was started in 1988 in Massachusetts. All of them help ex-convicts get back on their feet. Contact: www.dismas.org or www.dismashouse.org.

### FedCURE

FedCURE is the CURE chapter for federal prisoners and families. Contact: fedcure.org.

### Goodwill Industries

Nonprofit Goodwill Industries prepares ex-convicts for the workforce. They provide mentoring and shelter and help ex-convicts secure jobs and remain in them. Contact: www.goodwill.org.

### Inside-Out Program

Started at Temple University with the assistance of the Philadelphia Prison System, the program brings selected college students into local prisons to teach inmates. This program has expanded nationally. Contact: www.temple.edu/inside-out.

### Inviting Convicts to College: Convict Criminology

A program based at the University of Wisconsin at Oshkosh, Department of Public Affairs. The program includes Convict Criminology courses taught by undergraduate student teachers inside a number of medium- and maximum-security prisons in Wisconsin. Contact: www.convictcriminology.org/college.html.

### Narcotics Anonymous

Originators of the self-help program for drug addicts. When you go to their website, you can type in your location and find a nearby meeting. Contact: www.na.org.

## Open Inc.

A private company that markets self-help books to the prison system. Contact www.openinc.org.

## Prisoner Visitation and Support (PVS)

Established in 1968, PVS is an interfaith organization that organizes local people to visit federal prisoners all over the United States. Contact: www.prisonervisitation.com.

## Project Rebound

A program for ex-convicts who want to go to college at San Francisco State University. Started by ex-convict professor John Irwin during the late 1960s. Contact: www.sfsu.edu/~rebound.

## Salvation Army

Religious-based organization that may have a list of local employers who hire parolees. They also run halfway houses, shelters, and food pantries; serve meals; and provide temporary employment. They also donate clothing and bus tickets to those in need. Contact: www.salvationarmyusa.org.

## The Society of St. Vincent de Paul

Religious-based organization that operates programs in many state prisons to help prisoners and recently released convicts. They also hire formerly incarcerated people. Programs and services are not coordinated on a national basis. A person needs to contact the local organization to find out what they have to offer. Some groups meet prisoners as they walk out the prison gates. Most of their thrift centers may offer free clothes, furniture, and even money to help ex-convicts pay the rent. Contact: www.svdpusa.org.

## Volunteers of America

This national nonprofit faith-based organization runs programs all over the United States. Some of these services include halfway houses, drug treatment programs, and back-to-work programs for convicts. Contact: www.voa.org.

# Appendix C

## Books to Keep on Your Night Table

Looking for some further reading? Try any of the following titles:

Bolles, Richard Nelson. *What Color Is Your Parachute? 2009: A Practical Manual for Job-Hunters and Career-Changers.* Berkeley California: Ten Speed Press, 2008.

Gonnerman, Jennifer. *Life on the Outside.* New York: Picador, 2005.

Krannich, Ron. *The Ex-Offender's Job Hunting Guide.* Manassas Park, VA: Impact Publications, 2005.

Maruna, Shadd. *Making Good: How Ex-Convicts Reform and Rebuild Their Lives.* Washington, D.C.: American Psychological Association, 2001.

Maruna, Shadd, and Russ Immarigeon, eds. *After Crime and Punishment: Pathways to Offender Reintegration.* Portland, OR: Willam, 2004.

Miller, Jerome G. *Search and Destroy: African-American Males in the Criminal Justice System.* New York: Cambridge University Press, 1996.

Milligan, Edie. *Blindsided: Financial Advice for the Suddenly Unemployed.* Indianapolis, Alpha Books, 2001.

O'Brien P. *Making It in the Free World.* Albany, NY: State University of New York Press, 2001.

Owen, Barbara. *In the Mix: Struggle and Survival in a Women's Prison*. Albany, NY: SUNY Press, 1998.

Parenti, Christian. *Lockdown America*. London: Verso, 1999.

Peterscilia, Joan. *When Prisoners Come Home: Parole and Prisoner Reentry*. New York. Oxford University Press, 2003.

Ross, Jeffrey Ian. *Special Problems in Corrections*. Upper Saddle, NJ: Prentice Hall, 2008.

Ross, Jeffrey Ian, and Stephen C. Richards. *Behind Bars: Surviving Prison*. Indianapolis, Alpha Books, 2003.

Ross, Jeffrey Ian, and Stephen C. Richards, eds. *Convict Criminology*. Belmont, CA: Wadsworth Press, 2003.

Shelden, Randall G. *Controlling the Dangerous Classes: A Critical Introduction to the History of Criminal Justice*. Boston: Allyn & Bacon, 2001.

Travis, Jeremy. *But They All Come Back: Facing the Challenges of Prisoner Reentry*. Washington, D.C.: Urban Institute Press, 2005.

Travis, Jeremy, and Christy Visher, eds. *Prisoner Reentry and Crime in America*. New York: Cambridge University Press, 2005.

# Index

# C